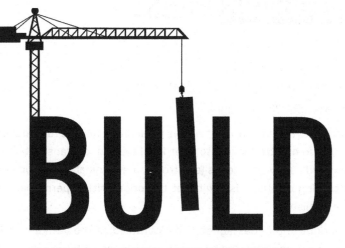

BUILD

HOW TO CREATE PRIVATE WEALTH AS A SUCCESSFUL **PROPERTY DEVELOPER**

JIM CASTAGNET

RETHINK PRESS

First published in Sydney 2017
by Rethink Press (www.rethinkpress.com)

© Copyright Jim Castagnet

Cover images © Katie Bell and James Weston

CONTENTS

Introduction 9

My Background 13

CHAPTER 1: PROPERTY DEVELOPMENT DEFINED

What is property development? 17

The Seven Deadly Mistakes in property developing 18

So how do we get it right? 22

Why do property development? 22

Does it take a 'special breed' to become a successful
  property developer? 23

Is it for me? 25

CHAPTER 2: THE PROPERTY DEVELOPMENT CAKE

The ingredients: elements of property development 27

How to make the cake 28

CHAPTER 3: HERE'S WHERE YOU MAKE THE MONEY

Sourcing development sites 33

Sites made to order 36

CHAPTER 4: WHAT'S NORTH GOT TO DO WITH IT?

Site analysis 43

CHAPTER 5: CREATING THE DEAL

The financial feasibility analysis 45

Total Development Costs 48

Your feasibility analysis tool 49

CHAPTER 6: WHAT THE HELL WAS I THINKING?

Risk analysis and management 51
Site sourcing 52
Site acquisition and negotiations 54
Development approval process 57
Funding 62
Tendering for a builder 63
Construction 67

CHAPTER 7: IF IT'S NOT A WIN/WIN, IT'S NOT HAPPENING

Site negotiations and acquisitions 79
The purchase price 84
Option fee 85
Option period 86
Terms and conditions 87

CHAPTER 8: DANCE OF THE SEVEN VEILS

Joint ventures 89
JVs with landowners 90
Syndicates 91
Investor proposals 92

CHAPTER 9: HOW TO GET YOUR APPROVAL – *FAST*

The development approval process 95
Concept development 99
Pre-lodgement 99
Lodgement of the development application 100
Referrals 102
Notification 102
Assessment 102
Determination 103
Construction Certificate (Building) Approval 105
Summary 105
How and where to find assistance 107

CHAPTER 10: PROPERTY DEVELOPMENT IS A TEAM SPORT

Choosing your team: the role of consultants 109

CHAPTER 11: FINDING BOB

Tendering for the builder 115
Negotiated contract 119
Managing the construction process 120

CHAPTER 12: PROTECTING YOUR ASSETS

Structures for property development and
   other legal issues 123
My preferred structure 126

CHAPTER 13: SHOW ME THE MONEY

Property development finance 129
Funding structure 131
Financial modelling and funding 133

CHAPTER 14: HOW THE BANK ASSESSES YOUR FUNDING SUBMISSION

Debt servicing 143
Cash flow forecast 146
Cash flow forecasts – borrower/guarantor/sponsor 148
Management/management information systems 149
Customer rating system and risk profile 151
Commercial property development lending –
   specific guidelines 153
Property/project risk and competitive position 153
Property market and other risks 157
Quality of securities 158
Securities for commercial property development
   lending – specific guidelines 159
Minimum security requirements 161
Conditions precedent 162

Covenants/ratios disciplines/conditions 165
Covenants for commercial property development
    lending – specific guidelines 167
Exit analysis 168

CHAPTER 15: IT HAS TO SELL ITSELF
Marketing your project 171

CHAPTER 16: HOW AND WHEN DO I GET OUT?
Exit strategies 175

CHAPTER 17: THE PROOF OF THE PUDDING IS IN THE EATING
The Apprentice Property Developer Masterclass 179

SUMMARY
Getting Started 186
Your Property Development Business Plan 186
Interview With Jim Castagnet, Author, MD and
    Founder, Property Development Workshops 188

Acknowledgements 193
The Author 194

This book is dedicated
to Marie-Louise Claudine Castagnet.
Your kindness, love, dedication and
sacrifices will never be forgotten.
You will always be a queen to me.

INTRODUCTION

Property development is the most lucrative business in the world. It is this very fact that draws many to try their hand at it. It is not for the faint-hearted, however, or for those who are ill-prepared or uneducated in this particular field. So let me congratulate you for taking the first step in your journey by reading this book.

A myriad disciplines contribute to the knowledge base of the successful property developer. You will need to know about architecture, engineering, public relations, industrial relations, property finance, property law, construction, accountancy, general management, sales and marketing, communications, town planning, valuation, quantity surveying and land surveying, to name just a few.

So where do you find all this information? Practically, of course, you cannot go to university to obtain a degree in each of these disciplines.

In this book I would like to share with you how I made my transition from senior executive in the corporate world of telecommunications to full-time property developer. The journey has not been an easy one, and you certainly do not have to travel the same rocky road that I took in order to become successful.

One of the biggest obstacles I struck when starting out back in 1998 (and little has changed in this regard since, I believe) was the problem of finding quality advice and information from experienced developers who knew what they were talking about. They were either too busy, bound by confidentiality agreements, or just unwilling to share their hard-earned and costly lessons with potential competitors. It's the 'secret sauce' syndrome. It really can be the most guarded of industries when it comes to getting practical advice. Which is one of my reasons for writing this book.

When I was doing my research, I found only three books, two by the same author, that more or less addressed property development directly. The authors were not developers, though, but rather had worked as consultants on development projects. Being a development consultant to the actual developer is like being a chef in a restaurant owned by someone else. The risk profile is vastly different. For the developer, the decision-making process at the holistic level is much more demanding. Only the business owner bears the brunt of all the risks of that business and, more importantly, has the power to make the business succeed or fail.

This book presents invaluable knowledge and a step-by-step guide to orchestrating all the necessary elements that make up property development. I will introduce you to my own Property Development Process through a framework that takes you through the seven phases of a property development project.

The book provides a practical guide and a blueprint for any development project you are likely to undertake. Like the DNA from which an infinite variety of life forms are created, once mastered, the information and knowledge you accrue can be applied repeatedly to creating wealth through property development. I promise you an exciting journey, so enjoy the ride.

MY BACKGROUND

I arrived in Australia at the age of eleven through the migrant gateway of Sydney's inner western suburbs. My father, who had been a primary school teacher in Mauritius all his life, had secured a job at the De La Salle Brothers Catholic School in Sydney. It was my first experience of Australian culture.

I remember my very first day at high school. The teacher had asked, 'And what would you like to do when you grow up?' The kids rattled off the usual suspects: fish and chip shop owner, builder, policeman, accountant... No one, as I recall, volunteered 'property development' as an ambition! Indeed, right through school and university, and my eighteen years in the corporate world, I had absolutely no clue of the existence of the property development industry.

Given that this is not just any industry, but one that affects each and every one of us in some way, and has the power to drive the whole Australian economy (although not necessarily in a positive direction), it is surprising that the average person – that's 99.9% of us – knows nothing about property development, let alone its career potential.

Property development is the driving force behind count-less businesses, and in particular our retail industry. Think about the run-on effects of building a block of apartments. You will have provided employment for thirty or more consultants and public servants. At the same time, retailers of building materials, furniture and fittings such as carpets, tiles, taps, paint, curtains, beds, dining tables and chairs, kitchens and bathrooms, electrical goods, electronic devices and many other products will benefit either directly or indirectly from your venture.

I remember working on a seven-apartment development in Bellevue Hill in Sydney's Eastern Suburbs. We used to have our weekly site meetings at Birriga's Café at the end of the street. The builders and subbies would always buy their morning tea and lunches there too. We even held Melbourne Cup lunches there. To the delight of the café owner, who became a good friend, the development went on for much longer than expected. When we completed the project and moved on, the café suffered a severe downturn in business and almost went under. That was fifteen years ago, and I am happy to report that Birriga's Café is still going strong.

What became apparent to me, though, was the importance of my development project to the community as a whole. In fact, what I do now when assessing a property development venture is to make a list of all the stakeholders and then learn who they are and how they might be affected, positively or negatively, by my venture. This exercise is vital to establishing my approach to my development and, indeed, to evaluating the project's potential for success.

Chapter 1

PROPERTY DEVELOPMENT DEFINED

What is property development?

The *Collins English Dictionary* defines property development as 'the business of buying land and buildings and then making improvements to them so that their selling price exceeds the price paid for them'. Sounds simple enough. So why do so many get it so wrong? I hope not only to solve that mystery in this book, but also to show you how to do it successfully time after time.

Let's begin by identifying the most common mistakes that property developers make.

The Seven Deadly Mistakes in property developing

Property developers are by nature entrepreneurs and risk takers. They are enthusiastic and passionate individuals who are generally successful at what they do. However, those very characteristics that make them successful can often cause them to make unnecessary and costly mistakes. During the eighteen years I have been teaching and practising property development, I have found these to be the seven most common mistakes that property developers are prone to in their haste to make things happen.

Mistake no. 1: lack of due diligence. A thorough due diligence process is an absolute must if you are to reduce your risks as a property developer. The scope of this process will depend on the complexity of your particular project. Rookie developers will often do the bare minimum of what is necessary. They will commit to purchase on the word of an often unqualified third party. If you're unsure of what is needed, I recommend you commission a qualified consultant to do this work for you. It will help you to avoid costly mistakes and hidden pitfalls, and could save you thousands.

Mistake no 2: massaging the financial feasibility. The feasibility analysis is the most critical element of your due diligence. If you get this wrong, you will probably end up overpaying for the land or walking away from a perfectly viable project. The Feasibility underlies everything that you do. It will allow you to determine the residual value of land, and therefore how much to pay (which ideally should be below the residual value).

A problem I see time and time again is that developers tend to overestimate the sales of their projects while underestimating the construction costs. It is too easy to play with the figures to support the outcome you want rather than clearly reflect the reality. What often happens then is that the developer goes ahead and purchases the site, and spends loads of money on getting development approval (DA), only to find that the project does not stack up, so the bank won't fund it. Which is why there are so many sites on the market that are simply not viable.

Mistake no. 3: underestimating the power of neighbours. Neighbours need to be on your list of stakeholders who are affected by your development. Very often lots of anxiety is created unnecessarily because the developer has surprised the neighbours with the proposed development, having failed to communicate their intentions to these interested parties prior to lodging the DA application. Remember that the fewer objections received by the council, the easier it will be to get your DA. Neighbours are also constituents who vote for their local councillors, so their concerns do carry weight when the council is considering your application. They can hold up your application interminably. Worse still, they can force you to take the matter to the Land and Environment Court, where you will face even more delays and court costs.

Mistake no. 4: selecting the wrong builder. There is nothing more heartbreaking than having the builder go broke halfway through your project. It is very costly to replace a builder and your budget may not be sufficient to do so without further injection of funds. Builder selection is a critical part of the property development process, and too often a builder is selected based on a recommendation from a mate or on the cheapest price. Depending on the size of your project, it is wise to use the services of a quantity surveyor, who will be able to provide cost estimates for your project when assessing the builder's tender. They can also advise on the performance of particular builders as they are often processing monthly progress payments on the bank's behalf. They know the builders who perform on time and on budget.

Mistake no. 5: shoddy legal documentation. This is an issue that is often overlooked by even the most experienced developers. Indeed I have been guilty of getting this wrong myself, and it has been very costly. There are obvious reasons to ensure that your legals – by which I mean option agreements, joint ventures, non-disclosure agreements, building contracts, pre-lease agreements and a host of other formal structures and provisions, depending on your situation – are up to scratch. These include minimising your liabilities and protecting your assets to ensure you get to keep your profits at the end. If you don't engage a qualified property development solicitor and accountant who can advise in this regard, you risk being exposed before, during and/or after the completion of your project.

Mistake no. 6: not selecting the right consultant. It's worth reminding yourself of the truism that 'if you pay peanuts, you get monkeys'. To succeed in property development you need to surround yourself with the right team, including the right architect, solicitor, accountant, town planner and quantity surveyor. Too often developers opt for the cheapest consultants, and inevitably this costs them more in the long run. Mistakes result in variations and an inferior end product. At the end of the day, the developers don't achieve the *highest and best use*, which of course results in less profit – or even a loss.

Mistake no. 7: buying the wrong site. This is the most common mistake I see developers make. There can be many explanations for this, including lack of due diligence and incorrect or incomplete (back of the envelope) feasibilities. Often it comes down to a combination of lack of knowledge and understanding of the property development process in relation to buildability issues, funding, planning framework and/or the target market. The risk with property development most often lies not in the project itself but in the property developer. Self-education in property development is a critical part of a developer's due diligence.

So how do we get it right?

The key word in the above Collins Dictionary's description of property development is *business*. I have come to realise that property development is not about undertaking a one-off project. It is a business that can involve one or multiple projects, but like any business it needs a CEO or managing director. Someone who is in charge, but more importantly someone who is responsible and accountable for the success of the business. And that person is *you*. If you are to succeed in property development, you must empower yourself and make happen.

By definition, if you're going to start a business, you will need the necessary skills to manage *the business*, and not just a construction project. Indeed, many newcomers to the industry are pleasantly surprised to learn that they already possess a number of the skills they will need to succeed as a property developer. They just need to learn how to apply those skills to the new task.

Why do property development?

Property development is truly one of the most rewarding industries in the world, and one of the most effective pathways to creating lasting wealth. Some 75% of the top 200 BRW rich-listers hold their wealth in property.

When practising property development, you are obligated to make substantial profits on each project. Indeed, if you cannot do so you will not be able to secure the funding required to proceed with the project.

A word of caution, however. Although if you get it right the money will flow as it is but a measure of a job well done, I wouldn't focus solely on making money. Rather, concentrate on honing the skills required to deliver each phase of your development, being aware and respectful of all stakeholders and sensitive to the environment.

Making a good profit, or even a super profit, is important. I believe your true reward, though, is the sense of fulfilment and satisfaction you will enjoy when you complete this challenging task successfully. What's more, you will earn the respect of your peers and the community when you make positive contributions to society and to the economy.

Does it take a 'special breed' to become a successful property developer?

I once spent three years in the Land and Environment Court doing battle with the local council over a stormwater easement through the neighbours' property (which I will discuss in more detail later in this book). I remember asking my solicitor, who was an expert on the Court and very knowledgeable about planning matters, if he had ever considered taking up property development himself.

His answer was a respectful, 'No, it's not for me. It takes a special breed of person to do property development.' I will leave it to you to make up your own mind on that as you work through this book and your own projects. In a later chapter we look more closely at the qualities and attributes needed and why *you* hold the key to success.

Suffice to say here that a successful developer commands a lot of respect, and personally I have found it to be a profoundly fulfilling profession on many levels. As a business leader, I believe I can contribute to society and be a positive influence for the community. I provide employment and serve as an educator while creating a legacy for my family. Property development for me is at the exciting 'pointy end' of entrepreneurship.

The property developer is a visionary who creates development opportunities, orchestrates processes and manages consultants to turn that vision into reality. Ten developers will look at one site and come up with ten different solutions for how to use it. There is no right or wrong answer, except of course if a proposal cannot be approved by the council. Each solution will have a different outcome and, importantly, a different profit (and therefore risk) margin.

The best developer strives to achieve *the highest and best use* for a site. Often, the most successful developer is the one who sees opportunity where no one else does, and who will therefore achieve a better outcome than anyone else.

Is it for me?

If you're interested in fast-tracking your wealth creation and looking to create a legacy for your retirement and your family, then consider property development as one of the strategies, if not *the* strategy for achieving your goals.

Now, take this quick quiz:

☐ Are you aprofessional or corporate executive, earning a salary and perhaps working up to sixty hours a week?

☐ Would you like to free up your time and create wealth at the same time so you can control how long and when you work?

☐ Would you like to start making huge profits, without leaving your current job?

☐ Are you a small business owner wishing to create another more lucrative income stream?

☐ Are you a property investor ready to embrace a more proactive strategy to speed up your wealth creation?

☐ Would you like to ensure that you are creating profits and wealth while exposing your business to minimum manageable risk so your and/or your family's assets are protected?

☐ Would you like to learn the tightly guarded strategies that successful developers and entrepreneurs use?

☐ Would you like to enter the property development industry using little or none of your own money?

If you have answered yes to most of the questions, then you are probably ready to take your next step to becoming wealthy through property development.

Chapter 2

THE PROPERTY DEVELOPMENT CAKE

The ingredients: elements of property development

Over many years of practising and teaching property development I have determined the main elements that make up each project. This framework has greatly facilitated the learning process for my students. Identifying and working through each of these eight elements systematically will allow you to attack the development process in a clear and methodical way. It will also make the whole process of communicating with and managing your team much easier.

Consider these your project milestones:

- Technical and financial feasibility analyses
- Legal structures for projects
- Property development finance
- Site acquisition/negotiations
- Development approval (DA) application process
- Tendering/construction
- Marketing and sales
- Exit strategies.

I have incorporated these eight elements into my Property Development Process

How to make the cake

The following flow chart simplifies the complex process by breaking it down into bite-size pieces. More importantly, it shows how tackling each phase of the process depends on you having completed the one before, like climbing a mountain one step at a time. Any attempt to cut corners or circumvent any of the steps in the process will inevitably come back to bite you sooner or later. Self-discipline in this regard is paramount if you're to succeed.

The Property Development Process

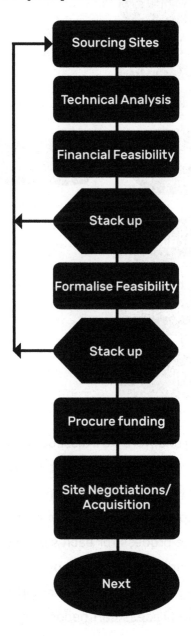

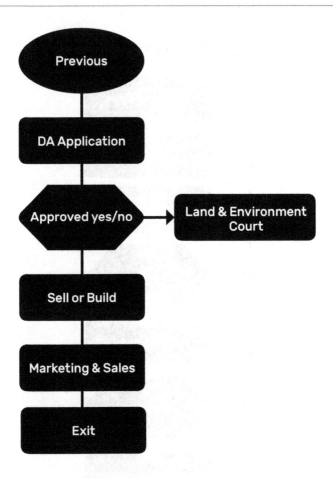

In the following chapters we'll dissect each of the seven phases in the Property Development Process so you can learn to complete each phase successfully. I should point out at this stage that you may not want to complete the whole of the process for each site. There are many potential exit points you might choose to make use of as you work through the process. And completing a particular part of the process can become in itself a niche business that you can undertake to generate relatively quick and often substantial cash flow to start your own development business.

Mastering the Site Sourcing and Acquisition steps in the flow chart will enable you to source and create outstanding development sites and on-sell them to other property developers who are geared to take on the construction phase of the process. This 'early harvest' will allow you to start your property development business quickly by generating cash flow without having to invest lots of money.

Chapter 3

HERE'S WHERE YOU MAKE THE MONEY

Sourcing development sites

You make your profit when you secure the site. It is at this point that many would-be developers fail. They purchase the wrong site, for the wrong reasons, at the wrong price and in the wrong location.

In my workshops I always ask participants to list on a sheet of butcher's paper where they go to source a development site, and invariably the same answers come up:

real estate sites on the internet, newspapers, real estate agents, word of mouth, family and friends.

This is what you do when you look for a site *passively*. In other words, you're waiting for someone to put a site up for sale, and you're hoping it's the right one for you. And if it's not quite what you want, against your better judgement you may try to adjust your business plan to fit, because you are anxious to start developing. I can tell you that this will absolutely increase your risks and your chances of failure.

Apart from the fact that the site is now on the open market and you will have to compete on price with other bidders, perhaps at auction, there is a reason why the site is for sale in the first place. And often it is not a good reason. Let's face it, if the site is a 'cracker' that is going to make lots of money, why is it being sold? Don't get me wrong, not every site on the market is a 'dog', but you have to do your due diligence and make sure there are no technical or other hidden issues.

For example, if it is a DA-approved site, the conditions of consent may be onerous and require costly resolutions that make the site unviable. Most sites for sale that I have assessed are not fundable. In other words, the owner has not been able to secure the necessary finance to do the construction. This is a huge red flag. Despite all the complaints about how hard it is to get development funding from the bank, these harsh criteria do provide us with the comfort of knowing that if a bank is willing to fund a project, it will be relatively safe.

A colleague of mine sold his cold storage business. Cashed up, he started looking for something new to do and he decided to give property development a go.

'There was a block of land of approximately 10,700 square metres for sale and I bought it,' he told me later in a phone call. I asked him why he bought that particular site and his answer was, 'It was cheap.'

It turned out he had bought a light industrial site in South Nowra, in regional New South Wales. He had managed to get development approval for a five-site subdivision, which he intended to sell. But after some three years on the market, he could not find one person interested in buying any of the sites. Hence his call to me. In the meantime, the DA required him to raise the level of the site to guard against flooding and to put in sealed roads and gutters. By now the site, which he had bought for $500,000, had cost him $900,000.

To add to his woes, he is not a resident of the area and has had to travel to the site countless times to resolve issues. Sadly, at the time of this book being written, he still has not been able to offload the site, not even below cost, and the interest is clocking up.

It would be remiss of me not to acknowledge that the global financial crisis did not help matters. We will be talking about external risks later in the book.

To run a business (remember, you're running a property development *business*), you have to be able to control how and when you pay out and the amount of money you are prepared to spend to make money. The best development sites never make it to the market. So what I would like to share with you is how you can *proactively* source property development sites based on your own predetermined criteria. I want to introduce you to my proven system for locating the best development sites, which I call the Development Site Sourcing Funnel.

Sites made to order

When you're sourcing a development site, it is fundamental you obtain one that you have 'designed' for your own requirements. In other words, you need to decide the specific purpose for the site – for example, as a luxury residential development, a mixed-use development in a town centre, or a commercial or industrial development.

It is critical that you master this *predetermined criteria* method, because what I will show you is how you can 'take orders' from clients seeking sites and fulfil them to make your own very profitable site acquisition business. Your clients might include, for example, other developers, corporate clients or construction companies who are geared to build and are looking for sites that meet specific criteria in predetermined locations. More on this later.

As a matter of course you will need to set a budget, and you need not be limited by your own bank account here, as I will discuss later in the book. You will also want to pick a location that you would like to be active in developing.

One of the givens for me is to know your patch. Pick a location to which you have ready access, perhaps near where you live or in the next town or municipality, then get to know it like the back of your hand.

You will know what's selling, for how much and so forth at any given time. You will know all the real estate agents who work the area, and you will be familiar with the local council, the councillors and the information on their website. Even the local rag is a great source of information. You can be sure that if any controversial developments are proposed in the area, the story will make the local paper. In addition, the council is obliged to advertise any proposed development according to criteria defined in their Local Environment Plan (LEP).

Here's how my Development Site Sourcing Funnel™ works.

Locating the ideal site

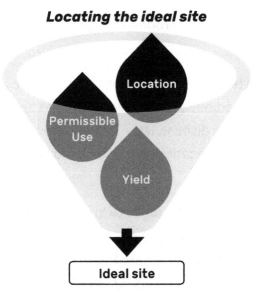

From a more practical point of view, here's the process you will go through to find your ideal site quickly.

The Development Site Sourcing Funnel™

Location

Zoning (e.g B4, R4)

Yield: Floor Space Ratio (FSR) or building envelope (e.g. 4:1 FSR)

Height, Set backs

Affecters (e.g. flooding, heritage, acid sulphate soil, Aboriginal land)

Feasibility Analysis

This identifies the three areas you need to focus on when locating your ideal site:

Location Choose your location (consider proximity and access, the type of development you want to do, target market, budget, zonings, imminent LEP changes, government policies, etc.).

Permissible use Go to the council website and access the planning maps. The Land Use Map will show you the zonings within your location. Remember, we're after the high density zonings for residential and/or mixed use (commercial and residential) development.

Yield Now access the density map (FSR) and height maps. Pick the areas with the greatest density and building height.

Once you have narrowed it down to the specific areas, streets and sites with the highest densities and height allowances, check those sites for any affecters. In other words, check for any issues that might affect the land, including those listed above. I would disregard any that are heritage listed, for example.

By now you will have focused your search on, say, a particular street and a few suitable sites on that street.

Now narrow it still further, perhaps to three or four sites, depending on the size of the land parcel and whether you may have to amalgamate to make a bigger site.

At this point you will probably need to take a drive and do a site inspection to identify any issues, positive or otherwise, that might affect the sites you are assessing. Those issues could include exposure to traffic, proximity to schools and transport, other similar developments in the area, site orientation and of course views.

I am fortunate to live in the beautiful city of Sydney, where the harbour really dominates local planning rules and guidelines. Aside from the views, which the residents will do anything to protect, there are strict guidelines on the bulk and scale of development around the harbour foreshore.

Recently a major development company went into liquidation while trying to develop a significant site in the harbour-side suburb of Double Bay. They had badly underestimated the determination of the local residents to resist overdevelopment. Knowing your planning guidelines and, importantly again, the stakeholders and general local conditions and feel of the area will be invaluable to you. We will cover this in more detail in the 'Site analysis' section in the following chapter.

Once you have considered the physical attributes of the sites and have selected one or two, you will want to carry out a financial feasibility analysis. This will determine the project's viability and the Residual Land Value of the site. Residual Land Value is quite different from the market value of the land. If you have done your homework, typically it will be considerably higher than the market value, which is why you can offer the landowner a better deal than even the most enthusiastic real estate agent could. It is also why you are able to obtain an Option agreement from the landowner.

The call option, by the way, is the best way a developer can acquire land, as I will discuss in detail in the section 'Site negotiations and acquisitions' later in the book.

But how do you know your perfect site is even for sale? My answer is simple. *Every* site is for sale.

Chapter 4

WHAT'S NORTH GOT TO DO WITH IT?

Site analysis

Once you have located a particular site you are interested in, you will need to undertake a Technical Site Analysis as part of your due diligence. In due course you will require the assistance of your architect and other consultants, such as the land surveyor and geotechnical engineer, as any site may potentially contain in-ground risks. However, before determining whether you want to go further with the site, you can do some initial analysis yourself.

The following are some of the basic issues to consider:

Check the site's orientation. Is it facing north? A north-facing site (or south-facing if you live north of the equator) has a great advantage when you are designing your development, as it will be much easier for you to achieve the required energy ratings to gain DA approval.

Are there any significant trees on the site? The council may not allow the removal of certain trees, which may be heritage listed. Depending on their location, large trees can pose significant buildability issues as well as reducing the overall yield for a site.

The depth of the water table. This can be problematic if you're considering basement car parking.

Privacy. Are there issues relating to overlooking neighbours' properties?

Each site will be different, and this list is by no means exhaustive. The financial impact of any technical issues must be taken into account in the financial feasibility analysis.

Chapter 5

CREATING THE DEAL

The financial feasibility analysis

For the accountants out there, the financial feasibility analysis (the Feasibility) is simply a profit and loss statement. The difference is that it's not a financial statement of what has already occurred but a snapshot of what you believe will be the outcome of your venture, based on today's costs and selling price.

The Feasibility is the most critical element of your due diligence. If you get this wrong, you will probably end up either overpaying for the land or walking away from a perfectly viable project. Be careful to avoid 'paralysis by analysis': you do not want to be so conservative that you find reasons to throw out every potential project. On the other hand, if you are too enthusiastic you may be tempted to massage the figures to produce the result you want rather than reveal the reality. In this way you may end up with a project that is not viable and will cost you valuable time and money.

All the decisions you make should be based on the Feasibility. It will allow you to determine the residual value of the land you want to acquire, and therefore how much you would be willing to pay, which is not necessarily the actual residual value. Remember that if you have done your homework well and selected the right site, the residual should always be more than the property's market value. It is this that allows you to acquire property that is not on the market. More on this in the 'Site negotiations' section.

A number of off-the-shelf feasibility models allow you to fill in the fields and automatically calculate the outcome. Some of these models are very good, and you may well want to purchase one in the future. However, it is critical that you learn how to do a feasibility analysis organically and understand all the sensitivities involved before you start using an off-the-shelf modelling program. It is too easy to put figures into a spreadsheet that someone else has built and manipulate it to produce figures that may look good, but are totally misleading. Remember: garbage in, garbage out.

I recommend that you build your own feasibility spreadsheet using Excel, which will require you to input your own formulae. This is how you learn to appreciate the sensitivities and the relationships between the figures you input. It is a skill you will require to be able to create not only financial feasibilities but funding models to determine the source and application of funds.

A summary of a financial feasibility analysis may look as simple as the one shown here. It is often found in this format in the Executive Summary of an investor proposal or business case for funding.

Summary of simple financial feasibility analysis

FEASIBILITY ANALYSIS SUMMARY		
Revenue	Gross sales realisation, inc GST*	$ 26,405,519
	less: selling costs (net of GST)	-$ 532,828
	less: GST paid on ALL revenue	-$ 1,764,138
	Revenue net of GST and selling costs	$ 24,108,553

Development Costs net of GST	Land value	$ 7,000,000
	Development costs	$ 10,337,599
	Total Development Costs (TDC)	$ 17,337,599

Performance Indicators	Net development profit	$ 6,770,954
	Profit Margin (% of Development costs inc Selling Costs)	37.89%

*Goods & Services Tax

Essentially, as you can see, the formula used is simply:

Revenue – Cost of Goods Sold (COGS) = Profit

The example in the Financial Feasibility Study expands on the total development costs components in the summary.

Financial Feasibility Summary

FEASIBILITY ANALYSIS SUMMARY		
Revenue	Gross sales realisation, inc GST*	$ 26,405,519
	less: selling costs (net of GST)	-$ 532,828
	less: GST paid on ALL revenue	-$ 1,764,138
	Revenue net of GST and selling costs	$ 24,108,553

Total Develop-ment Costs	Land value	$ 7,000,000
	Stamp duty	$ 430,490
	Other acquisition costs	$0
	Total building costs	$ 7,511,931
	Total consultants' costs	$ 1,036,646
	Total building permit fees	$ 255,398
	Total on costs	$ 117,528
	Total finance costs, excl interest	$ 117,439
	Development costs, excl interest	**$ 16,469,433**
	Plus: Capitalised interest costs	$ 868,166
	TOTAL DEVELOPMENT COSTS	**$ 17,337,599**

Performance Indicators	Net development profit	$ 6,770,954
	Profit Margin (% of Development costs inc Selling Costs)	37.89%

Your feasibility analysis tool

A good feasibility analysis tool should provide the following:

■ Feasibility analysis snapshot summary, as shown above. (This assumes that all sales and development costs, including land, are at today's prices. Therefore no escalation has been allowed)

■ Cash flows for the duration of the project

■ Sensitivity analysis

■ Funding models, incorporating combinations of bank, external investors, landowners, developer

■ Costs of funds for any combination sources of finance (refer to section on 'Funding')

■ Source and application of funds table

■ Offer schedule for acquisition of land, showing the effect on profits for a combination of different offers to multiple landowners

■ Direct sales comparison table

■ Summary reports.

Chapter 6

WHAT THE HELL WAS I THINKING?

Risk analysis and management

My first project: *La Vie En Rose*, Bellevue Hill, Sydney NSW

This chapter focuses on risk by sharing some of the hard lessons I have learned over the years, including mistakes I do not let happen anymore.

Now I have to take you back a little to when I first started developing property full time. It was 1998 and this was my first project. This was me in your shoes right now, thinking I would love to take on a property development project. I did not have one ounce of knowledge about developing property, but I was keen.

I had just left an executive position as Regional Sales and Marketing Manager, Sydney, for one of Australia's biggest telecommunications companies, and I was ready for a new challenge. I was fortunate because, although I had left the company, I immediately contracted back to them and worked on as an independent consultant for another two years. This made my transition into a new career somewhat easier. I always urge students at my property development workshops to think about their business model and plan how they will either make a smooth transition into property development or incorporate property development as another income stream in their portfolio.

Site sourcing

So, back to my first project. The first thing I had to do was to find a suitable site. I remember walking into the office of a local real estate agency in Double Bay, one of the more affluent suburbs in Sydney, and approaching the woman behind the counter.

'I'm looking for a development site,' I stated plainly.

'How much are you looking to spend?' she asked.

'Well, about five or six hundred thousand dollars,' I replied.

'Not around here!' came the swift response. Bear in mind that this was 1998, when this was a significant amount of money.

Without the knowledge of how to source a development site (as outlined in Chapter 3), I drove around the municipality quite a lot over the next few weeks, until one day I came across a dilapidated old house for sale on top of a really steep block. Evidently it had been passed in at auction some time before and was just sitting there.

I thought it would be a perfect site for perhaps three or four townhouses. I called on an architect who had been introduced to me by one of my former direct reports in my previous job (note that this is *not* how to select your consultants). He did some rough sketches and thought we could put four townhouses on the block.

We turned up at the counter at Woollahra Council and spoke to the duty planner. Please understand that the person handling enquiries at the counter is normally the planner with the least practical experience whose training includes answering such walk-in enquiries.

So we discussed the concept designs with the planner, who concluded that we could not fit four townhouses on the block, or even three, once car parking spaces and turning circle were factored in. The council required two on-site parking spaces for each residence along with one visitor's spot for guests. Given the amount of excavation that would have to be done on this steep block of land, putting any fewer than four apartments on it would not have been viable, as I realised later.

Site acquisition and negotiations

Next I decided to approach the neighbour who lived in an old house on a similar block next door. If we could amalgamate the two blocks, perhaps the site could accommodate up to seven apartments.

To my pleasant surprise, the owners, an Asian couple, were very amenable to the idea of a joint venture agreement. Looking back on it now, I guess they were probably as naïve as I was with regard to property development, but that's not to say that they were a pushover when it came to negotiating the terms and conditions of our agreement.

The deal was for my entity to purchase their property subject to development approval from the council. Then both properties would be purchased simultaneously so the bank could take first mortgage security over them in providing the loan for the development. This was a great deal for both parties.

So what was the essence of the deal? What were the main terms and conditions that would make the neighbour agree to part with their property? What were their expected returns?

Well, here's what I agreed to give them in return for their property:

They had a mortgage of $248,000, which I agreed to pay off on settlement (amalgamation) of the land.

Rather than a financial payout as a return on their investment, they demanded a fully completed unit at the end of the project, to which I agreed. This apartment was a sub-penthouse. I had declined their request for the penthouse.

The lady of the house wanted the unit to be fully furnished, subject to an agreed budget of $46,000. Again, in 1998 that was a substantial sum of money.

The family consisted of Mr and Mrs Zao (not their real name) and their two school-age kids. However, the grandmother would visit from China every two or three months and would stay for a number of weeks at a time. I allowed them to redesign the floor plan into a four-bedroom apartment (although the bedrooms were smaller than the standard size). I agreed for them to pick their own finishes and fittings, to an agreed budget.

We agreed on minimum internal size for the apartment of 133 square metres.

As the block was steep and the old house was on the high end, they had quite good views over the surrounding valley and ocean glimpses. I agreed, naively, that their apartment in the new development would be at the same RL (relative level) as their old house so they could retain their views and outlook. Of course, when I announced this to the architect later, he nearly pulled his hair out, because he had to meet all the planning guidelines for height, setback, floor space ratio and so forth, as well as the challenges of a steep site and designing the seven-apartment development around this one apartment. This would come back to bite us later.

But wait, there's more. When construction began, the Zaos would have to move to new premises until completion. I agreed to pay their rent at $600 a week until they moved back into their new apartment.

In New South Wales all transactions where the title is transferred from one party to another entity incur stamp duty. I agreed to pay the stamp duty for transfer of their property into my entity and then again when the new apartment was transferred into their name. At approximately 5% of the value of the property, these were substantial amounts, as the original property was valued at $820,000 and the finished apartment at $1.7 million.

Finally, I agreed that I would finish the development within a fixed period of time or I would be liable for penalties to the value of $100,000, increasing on a pro-rata basis.

Believe it or not, this was still an exceptional deal for me, not least for the fact that as an inexperienced developer I had the opportunity to undertake a decent-size project that I was able to fund because of the equity that the two blocks provided.

Having said that, my original intention had been to start out small because of my inexperience. The reality was starting to hit home that I was about to take on a project that was at least three times the size of what I had expected and the risks had increased exponentially, not to mention that I now had an un-retractable responsibility to deliver a completed luxury apartment with all the trimmings to my joint venture partner. I was scared stiff, to say the least.

Development approval process

After I had secured the site, I briefed the architect on the type of development I wanted. He had worked out how we could accommodate six apartments with a penthouse on top, and basement car parking for all the apartments. I had done some research around Bellevue Hill and decided that a Tuscan style of architecture with sandstone features would be well received by the sophisticated target market in the area. It would need a medium to high level of finishes with polished floor-boards, designer kitchen and bathrooms with granite finishes, and large tiled balconies to capitalise on the views of the surrounding hills and valleys towards the north of Sydney Harbour.

Because the site was steep, the three upper levels of the five-storey building would benefit most from the views. Therefore my strategy to maximise the value of the development was to invest more in the upper levels by having the larger apartments there.

The architect used various books depicting Tuscany's classic architecture as inspiration when designing the building, and the landscape architect responded with appropriate landscape designs and planting, including a row of olive trees on the level one terrace. All this in the middle of Bellevue Hill in Sydney's Eastern Suburbs.

It was going to be interesting to see how the market would respond.

After about three months of design concepts and development, we lodged the development approval (DA) application with the council. The Zaos' apartment would be one of two sub-penthouses. The architect had advised that the approval process would probably take four to six months. I might just mention here that getting approval for a development from any council is generally a major challenge. This particular council was at the time one of the most litigious in the country.

As is normal protocol with these types of development, the council advertised the application for a period of two weeks to inform the community and allow time for any objections to be submitted. To our surprise, when the two weeks expired there were no objections from the neighbours. We speculated that because there had been quite a few developments in the street and the area generally – after all, that's what the land use zoning allows – the neighbours were fairly relaxed about yet another residential development.

I thought at that stage that the DA process should be fairly straightforward. There was no community resistance and the proposed development, while not totally compliant, was not controversial in any major way.

The architect called on the council every two weeks or so, as did I, to check on progress. As the weeks turned into months, we began to worry that our submission was deemed to be in some way unsuitable or inappropriate. I was having grave doubts by this stage, and while I was keeping the Zaos informed, I could offer no solid reasons for the delays.

Finally, after approximately six months, we heard from the Council Assessor. It turned out that because of the workload in the council at the time, he had not even looked at the application, which had been sitting there undisturbed for six months. He at last started his assessment, and the feedback we received was that there were a number of non-compliances that had to be addressed and various issues that the council was not happy about.

The one that was most concerning was that the building's height was approximately 1.5 metres above what the council would like. While we were within our height limit, because of the topography of the land we were actually higher than the existing development next door, and according to the council this would detract from the streetscape. They required me to bring down the height.

Other than the fact that it would reduce the views and outlook somewhat, this would not normally have been a problem. However, in the agreement I had with the Zaos, I had committed to building their new apartment *in the same space* as their old home. They were also very mindful of the effect the views, or the lack of them, would have on the value of the apartment. I had just started to realise the importance of any agreement made upfront and the effect it might have on the profitability or even viability of a project. In this instance, if I had to lose the penthouse in order to comply with the council's request to lower the height, then that would wipe out all the project's profit. Certainly the bank would not entertain financing it.

The architect had to find a way to reduce the height of the building without affecting the position of the Zaos' sub-penthouse apartment or impacting on the value of the development in any significant way. To my relief, he was able to bring the overall height of the building down while keeping within half a metre of the planned floor level for the Zaos' apartment, which was legally acceptable under our agreement. While we did lose some views, it was not a deal breaker.

We submitted the amended drawings to the council and the assessor was satisfied with the amendments. He advised that he would support the application in his report to the council. This would take about four weeks. We were approaching the end of the year and I decided that I would seize the opportunity to take my family on a holiday to Mauritius to visit relatives, returning in the New Year to start the new project.

In early to mid-January, while still on holiday, I got a call from the architect, who told me that the assessor had gone on 'indefinite leave' even though he had yet to complete his report.

'Not to worry,' I said. 'Who's taken his place? When will the report be completed?'

'No one is taking his place. The council's short staffed and there's no one available to replace him.'

Weeks later we got word from the council that they had decided to outsource some of their assessments to private planning consultants. Initially I thought this was good news. As it turned out, though, the planner who finally took up the assessment decided he did not like any of the work that had been done by the council planner. He advised that he was going to start the whole DA assessment process from scratch.

It was now some twelve months since we had lodged the original DA application and we were back to square one.

As a result of the changes required by the new planner, further amended drawings had to be done by the architect. By now this was costing me a lot of money in consultants' fees, not to mention the time delays.

After a further four months of to-ing and fro-ing, we finally got the DA approval from the council.

Never mind, I thought. I was now on my way.

The next step in the process was to have the architect produce the Construction Certificate drawings for approval. Not surprisingly, I lodged my application with a private certifier rather than with the council. It was approved within six weeks. The architect then created the tender drawings, which included detailed specifications so I could tender for a builder.

Funding

More importantly, at this stage I was able to obtain my bank loan, which had been pre-approved subject to DA, and settle on the blocks of land.

I had first addressed the funding question at the time I was contemplating entering the joint venture. My initial enquiries with the bank were very favourable. This was a time when the market was trending upwards and the banks were amenable to property development funding. The rules and criteria were much more lax, and indeed the banks used to lend up to two-thirds (66.6%) of gross realisations or end sales values. In those days, generally speaking, you would not require any pre-sales prior to starting construction.

More on funding later.

Tendering for a builder

Once the DA had been approved and the architect had completed the Construction Certificate and tender drawings, it was time to select a builder and start construction. Did I have any experience in running a construction project? No. So why was the bank happy to give a first-time developer a relatively large development loan?

When you're applying for development funding, the bank looks at two components. First, with the assistance of a valuer and a quantity surveyor, it assesses the viability of the project to ensure that it 'stacks up'. Second, it looks at the developer and his/her background to see what level of experience they possess. Often the biggest risk factor in a development project is not the project itself, but the developer.

In order to get funding, one of the criteria was that I would commission an experienced project manager to manage the construction phase. Indeed the bank representative recommended one for me, which at the time I thought was very helpful.

So I rocked up at the project manager's office and boldly announced, 'The bank sent me.'

Now what would the project manager have been thinking at this point? Probably he was rubbing his hands together, thinking all his Christmases had come at once. This is *not*, as you will see in a later chapter, how you select your consultants.

In any case, I took on the project manager, whom we'll call Dick (no, not his real name), on an exorbitant monthly retainer, which would be considered generous even by today's standards. And what would have been Dick's major role and responsibility at this point? He had to manage the tender process, select a competent builder at the right price, and secure a lump-sum fixed term contract, which is the only form of building contract the bank will accept for these types of developments.

Dick pulled out a list of ten or so builders for our perusal, from which he selected six that his firm had worked with in the past and that he thought would be suitable.

A comprehensive Tender Documentation package was compiled, including tender drawings from the architect and other major consultants as well as a set of specifications. This package was delivered to the six builders, who were given the standard four weeks to tender their submissions.

What I did not know at the time was that it is a must to hold mid-tender interviews to see how the builders are going with their pricing and to resolve any queries that may arise. I was now eagerly anticipating the arrival of a range of submissions, complete with prices, so we could make our selection and at last get on with construction. Four weeks went past, and how many submissions do you think we had received from the six tenderers? Zero is the correct answer. Instead we received requests for extensions, which we had little choice but to grant.

After the two-week extension had expired, how many had we received? Well, two. By the way, in granting funding for the project, the bank had accepted the quantity surveyor's costing of $2.2 million as total development costs, which was the figure used by the valuer when calculating the feasibility for the bank. My construction loan was therefore based on this estimate by the QS.

The quotes we got back from the two tenderers were $3.5 million and $3.25 million. That's more than $1 million over budget. I can tell you that at that time this was a significant amount of money.

I quizzed Dick the project manager at the time, but I can recall no plausible answer other than perhaps the builders had too much work on. He declared solemnly that I had two options. I could go through the tender process again, which would take another four to six weeks with no guarantee of success, or I could sit down and negotiate with one of the two builders and try to bring the price down. Dick suggested one of the builders as his preference, arguing that they were likely to be the hungrier of the two.

The negotiations would entail a 'Cost Engineering Workshop', Dick advised. I had no idea what he was talking about. He explained that this was the process for negotiating with the builder and the consultants to bring down the construction costs. Around the table at this workshop would be the builder, a new engineer recommended by the builder (who claimed he could bring down the structural costs by some $250,000), the architect, Dick, me, and a myriad of consultants, although they did not include the most important consultant from my point of view: the quantity surveyor. To this day I don't understand why the only person who could have challenged the builder on his prices was not present.

The workshop went on for weeks, with some of the consultants taking my side while others supported the builder in doing their utmost to keep the costs up. The structural engineer, recommended by the builder, had to be paid for his redesign, which was three times the price charged by the original engineer. As the workshop dragged on, the costs continued to mount up.

The real concern for me, though, was that while I was anxious to get the costs down, it was absolutely critical that the quality of the building, and therefore the value, was not compromised. This would certainly be detrimental in this high-end market, but more importantly, it could affect the bank's decision on funding. The bank had approved the funding based on the valuer's appraisal of the building as specified. To reduce the quality meant the valuer might have to revalue and adjust their figures accordingly. In turn, the bank could reduce their funding or, worse still, withdraw their funding altogether because the loan to value ratio had fallen outside their guidelines. So when the builder suggested 'bagging' the building rather than rendering it, alarm bells went off.

Finally, after four sessions, we agreed on a price of $2,650,000 for the construction. The architect and other consultants amended the drawings as required and a lump-sum fixed term/fixed price building contract was executed.

Construction

I was relieved and excited that we were now ready to start construction. The contract was for a period of fifty-two weeks. I couldn't wait to see the finished building.

The demolition of the two old houses on the site was completed in approximately three weeks. As the site was steep, contiguous piering was required along the boundary on three sides. At the back the piers were 12 metres deep. Since a great deal of excavation would have to be done, cost blow-outs were a real concern, and to mitigate that risk I had agreed with the builder on a fixed price for excavation. Needless to say, they had charged me a premium for this to cover their risks.

Once the piers had been poured, the next step was to anchor them so when the land was excavated, they would not be destabilised. This meant they had to be braced, and quite a few steel rods had to be inserted through the brace 6 or so metres below ground level and anchored into rock in the neighbours' properties. These temporary anchors would be removed after excavations were complete, but first I had to get the neighbours' written permission. The builder would not continue until I provided him with written advice.

You may recall that when I lodged the DA not one objection was received from any of the neighbours. So I imagined that obtaining their permission to insert the anchors, which are out of sight and are removed after approximately eight weeks, would be straightforward.

The property on the southern side was a rundown block of four apartments that was being leased as part of the affordable housing program. The owner lived in Canberra and we had never met. I wrote to her seeking permission for the anchors. The reply I received took me by surprise. Not only did she give me an emphatic 'No', but she declared that 'no amount of money would be sufficient' to persuade her to change her mind. Indeed, my offer of compensation reached $80,000 with no result.

Then out of the blue the apartment building was put up for sale for the ridiculously low amount of $595,000. Sadly I could not afford to buy it at that point, but a real estate agent living across the road from the property (no, not the listing agent) snapped it up. Seizing the opportunity for a quick turnover, she sold it almost immediately for $1.1 million. It sold again a year or so later for about $1.4 mil. After attempts to turn it into five apartments failed, it has now been redeveloped into two large luxury residences. The irony was that the previous owner who had been holding me to ransom was so uninformed about the value of property that she undersold it by some $500k. The new owner was happy to give permission for us to encroach into her property with the necessary rock anchors to enable excavation to proceed.

At the back of my project site was another larger run-down block of sixteen apartments. Again I had to obtain permission to insert temporary anchors in the property, but this time instead of dealing with one owner, I had to secure permission from a majority of sixteen different owners through their body corporate. This would be a challenge akin to herding cats.

Meanwhile the builder was doing nothing *and* sending me progress payment claims every two weeks for the delays. I had agreed in the building contract as a gesture of goodwill, and to make sure that the builder's cash flow was strong, that they could make fortnightly rather than monthly claims.

After I'd had a few meetings with the body corporate of the block of units at the rear, I realised it was obvious that they were in need of maintenance funds for their old property. The engineer came up with an offer for us to utilise much bigger contiguous piers than were required in order to give them support to build a car park at the back of their property, which would save them some $200,000 in ground works. The body corporate agreed and duly gave us permission to sink the anchors. To this day they have not built that car park, so the bigger piers were a total waste of money. Still, we were now ready to do the excavation and then begin construction.

Shortly afterwards I received a call from the project manager with further unwelcome news. He'd just learned from the builder that the excavation contractor had turned up on site that morning and was not happy. Having sized up the steepness of the site, he pointed out that my engineer had not prepared drawings for a ramp to allow the excavator to reach the top of the hill, so he promptly turned around and went home. (I found out later he had scored a more lucrative contract up the road.)

The reason the bank insists on a fixed term/fixed price contract is that the construction risks are carried by the party best able to deal with those risks, and that's the builder. Of course, the builder charges a premium for the privilege. In this instance all the subcontractors were commissioned by the builder and any failure on the part of subcontractors remained his responsibility. Nevertheless, he was determined to remain in dispute and continued to send through his fortnightly progress claims for delays. Since he had ceased to work, no other work was being claimed. The dispute went on for weeks, then months, and the claims continued to mount – to $500,000 and growing.

Then it all started to make sense. The building industry can be a small industry and news travels fast, especially among suppliers and subcontractors.

I received a call from the bank, asking me in for a meeting. They had another four developments on which this builder was working and they had become aware that he had gone into voluntary liquidation. However, they also recognised that my project remained viable. The piering and demolition had been completed, and they would support me while I replaced the builder.

After a big sigh of relief, I set about finding another builder. Around this time, however, a couple of things happened that turned this into an enormous challenge. In 2000 Sydney hosted the Olympic Games. This meant that by 1999 the construction trades were heavily engaged in building the sports stadiums and facilities to the absolute deadlines the Olympics demanded, and getting paid handsomely to do so. It was going to be difficult to interest any builder in taking on my project.

As if things were not bad enough, another major event happened around this time that almost brought me to my knees. Here's an excerpt from an article by Chas Keys, Deputy Director General, NSW State Emergency Service.

The response to the 'mother of all storms': a combat agency view

Early in the evening of Wednesday 14 April 1999, a massive hailstorm struck the southern, eastern and inner suburbs of Sydney. It produced colossal damage and over the ensuing weeks turned out to be, in insured damage terms, the most costly natural disaster ever to have occurred in Australia's history. A massive emergency response was mounted, lasting several weeks and giving temporary protection to many thousands of hail-damaged dwellings. Six months later the permanent repair work was still being carried out and while most roofs had been fixed the repairs to a minority of difficult cases were not expected to be finalised until well into the year 2000.

This once in a thousand years' hailstorm hit only one area hard: the Eastern Suburbs of Sydney. Yes, right in the area where I had started my first project. I also lived in the area and the roof of my house had collapsed during the storm. So it would be an understatement to say that at this point my wife and I were at the end of our tether.

But it got worse. Because now the bank called me in again. The manager informed me they had been advised by their head office in Queensland that they were 'overexposed' in Sydney's Eastern Suburbs, and unfortunately they were calling in the loan on my project. In other words, they were deserting me at the worst possible moment.

So I now found myself without a builder, without finance, with outstanding claims of $500,000 from my original builder and being chased by the liquidator, and penalty clauses in my joint venture agreement were about to kick in at $100,000 for each deadline missed. On top of that the family home was uninhabitable because of storm damage and the car looked like it had a bad case of measles from being peppered by hailstones. Thoughts of walking away did cross my mind, but I was absolutely determined to complete my first project and meet my commitments to my joint venture partner and the bank. I was in so deep I felt the only way out was to keep swimming to the other side.

Sorting out the previous builder's ambitious claim for half a million dollars was a priority. This was an added cost to my construction for works that had not been done. The builder had been trying to use the contract to put the squeeze on me. I was surprised how blatant he was.

Just before the liquidator was appointed, I received an invitation from the Managing Director of the construction company, which I won't name out of professional courtesy. He warned me they were going to be 'bloody-minded' about getting the $500,000 from me. But then he suggested another option:

'Give me $40,000,' he proposed, 'and while I am still in the Managing Director's chair I can get rid of the outstanding claims for $500,000.'

Naturally I flatly refused, and very much enjoyed doing so. I wish I had taped the conversation. I ran into the fellow some months later and he told me he had gone back to 'driving the ute' and trying to restart his career as a carpenter. A far cry from the flashy black Porsche and pretty young secretary in a big office.

Next thing I knew I found myself sitting in the boardroom at the liquidator's office, my barrister, Dr John Keogh, beside me and the liquidators glaring at us from the other side of the huge boardroom table, and I was expecting the worse. John is a doctor of law, mediator and arbitrator who knows his stuff. We walked away with a settlement for not 400, 300 or even 200k, but just $60,000. I remember as we walked out, John whispered that the liquidators 'just wanted to eat'.

I was ecstatic with the outcome as it meant that, other than the time lost, I had pretty much paid only for the demolition of the two old homes and the piling. The quantity surveyor had made sure we paid only for the work that had been done on the site; he had also ensured retention of 5% on each progress claim that had been paid. Hence the value of having the QS on board.

Meanwhile my new project manager, who had worked for some high-profile personalities in the area, had the foresight to undertake an early works package while we looked for a new builder. This set out all the excavations undertaken and completed, so the new builder could simply start on the superstructure and not have to worry about any ground work. Of course that saved on construction time.

We eventually found a builder and signed a twelve-month fixed term/fixed price contract. You will recall that the previous building contract was for $2.65 million. The new contract was negotiated for $2.2 million, and when the early works package for $165,000 was added, the total build contract amounted to $2.365 mil. I actually came out better off than with the first builder.

However, I had to refinance using a second tier lender and a second mortgage from a mezzanine lender (a hybrid between debt and equity finance) at a 35% interest rate. This is very expensive finance.

Construction had been going on for about two months or so when a young guy dropped by the building site and asked for the owner. Someone pointed me out and the guy came over and introduced himself. He said he was living in Bronte, the next suburb along, in a three-storey house and that he and his wife were expecting their second child. They were looking for a new place, preferably all on one level. He said he was interested in the penthouse in my development.

I showed him the plans and he said he was looking for something larger. I was very disappointed, and that night I was sitting in the lounge at home with my wife, discussing the plans and telling her how that pre-sale, although not a requirement by the bank at the time, would have been a blessing in many ways.

Then my son, who was twelve years old, said, 'Dad, why don't you join the two apartments on Level 3 and offer it to him?'

It was like a light had been turned on.

The next day my project manager, who had formerly been an architect, and I sat down and redesigned the two apartments into one massive residence with two large balconies. The buyer and his wife loved it and agreed to pay $1.910 million, which was top dollar at the time. This sale was in many respects my lifeline. It allowed me to go back to my first lender and increase my loan and use the funds to pay out the mezzanine lender. Although we had lost approximately four weeks in construction while we reconfigured the plans and obtained approvals, this sale essentially kept the project viable.

The builder completed the construction within the agreed time frame and the apartments sold quickly and for good prices. The Zoas received their completed, fully furnished apartment. I had escaped by the skin of my teeth.

While it would be easy for me to blame the council for delays, the neighbours for holding me to ransom, the builder for going broke, the consultants for taking advantage of my inexperience, the bank for calling the loan and indeed the acts of God, I have come to realise that at the end of the day I am, as the developer and project owner, fully responsible and accountable for everything that happens with my project.

With this realisation also comes the empowerment that being fully accountable brings and the fact that I can 'make happen' and I hold my destiny in my hands. This baptism by fire has made me who I am today and indeed the reason for establishing my property development education business and becoming a successful property developer.

Chapter 7

IF IT'S NOT A WIN/WIN, IT'S NOT HAPPENING

Site negotiations and acquisitions

You may have heard the old adage 'You make your profit when you do the deal'. Is it true? Well basically, yes, it is absolutely 'on the money', if you'll excuse the pun. So what does it *really* mean?

In Chapter 3, we discussed sourcing development sites based on your predetermined criteria. If you follow the prescribed funnel approach to locate your ideal site, you will probably choose one that is not for sale and therefore not advertised on the open market. The owner of the site is not even thinking about selling, let alone aware you're coming.

There are a number of reasons why this is the best way to acquire property. For one thing, there is no competition. Provided you have not posted it on Facebook or discussed it over a beer with your mates down at the pub, no one knows you're trying to acquire the site. At this point I do not recommend discussing it with anyone. Confidentiality is key.

To be successful at negotiating the best deal, you have to come at it from a position of strength and not fear. How do you achieve this? One of the most important things to remember is to go into it with a win/win mindset, not negotiating a deal that benefits you but screws the other person. If you have done your homework properly, you will approach the landowner confident that you are going to leave them better off than they were.

If, for instance, the owner is an elderly person, ask to speak with their adult children or their accountant or solicitor. When seeking a deal with any owner, always recommend that they obtain independent advice, particularly if it involves an option.

Before you can make an offer on a property, however, you need to determine how much you are willing to pay. So how will you determine this if the property is not for sale? Do not check with the local real estate agent – they won't know. You are not interested in paying market price; you will need to be able to pay well above market price. But how much above?

The range will be somewhere between market price and residual land value, and residual land value is determined by your own financial feasibility analysis.

Establishing this price range is also useful, for example, if you find yourself in desperate (and insane) need to buy a property at auction. It will ensure that you do not get emotionally carried away and overbid for the property.

As I write this, I am in the throes of negotiating a mixed-use site for which my corporate client has provided me with a pre-lease agreement. This is one way to operate from a position of strength. A pre-lease agreement creates massive notional value and will ensure you will be able to obtain funding. This gives you the confidence that, provided you obtain the property at the right price, you will make a super profit. About a week ago I delivered to the landowner a deed of option with terms and conditions, a contract of sale, a letter of offer to purchase for $24 million, a time frame within which to respond and a bank cheque for $50,000, representing the option fee. I am awaiting his response.

Do we have to be this clinical every time we negotiate a site? Perhaps not, but it pays always to be fully prepared.

Here's the negotiation process that I use to acquire property:

Do your financial feasibility. This document will be the basis for your decision-making process and everything you do in regard to your project, including applying for funding, budgeting, your baseline for cost management, pricing, discounting for pre-sales, the level of finishes, the overall quality of your project, your risk/reward assessment (hurdle rate) and of course what you are prepared to pay for the land.

Put yourself in the owner's shoes. Ask yourself whether *you* would be prepared to accept the offer you are about to make.

Arrange a meeting with the owner. Treat this as a fact-finding mission. You are not going to make an offer at this first meeting. It is an opportunity to find out the needs of the owner. Are they looking to retire and move up the coast in the next year or two? Are they downsizing because all the kids have left home? Do they want a new, maintenance-free residence while remaining in the neighbourhood close to their long-term friends or family? Are they cash flow poor and asset rich? Are there any financial issues such as Capital Gains Tax liabilities?

The answers to all these questions will shape the terms and conditions of your offer and help you to provide value to the landowner.

Arrange the next meeting. This is when you will deliver your offer in writing and allow a few days for review and consideration.

Follow up with meetings and negotiations. Achieve a heads of agreement (HOA) in which you and the landowner nut out, say, ten or so dot points that summarise the essence of your agreement.

Bear in mind that an HOA is not a legal document in itself, although there have been cases where it has been fought over in court. It makes it much easier (and cheaper) to convey to your solicitor exactly what has been agreed when he or she draws up the legal documentation. My experience is that once landowners have signed an HOA, they are psychologically committed to the deal. Often they will seek legal advice at HOA stage, therefore making the subsequent legal documentation easier and cheaper.

So what is it that we're negotiating exactly? In property development the goal in the first instance is not to own property, but rather to gain control of property while investing the least amount of money possible in order to minimise risks and holding costs. The best way to do that is by entering into an option agreement with the landowner. Here I want to focus on the call option, as opposed to the call and put option, which I do not recommend for novices – or indeed for anyone.

An option gives you the exclusive right, but not the obligation, to buy a property. Basically it comprises :

- The purchase price

- The option fee

- The time period to exercise the option.

In addition to these fundamentals, negotiate the terms and conditions. Often these are at least as important as the three primary components mentioned above.

I'll now explore the relationship between these components.

The purchase price

Be sure to do your homework before negotiating price with the owner. Remember that property owners these days are very sophisticated. They generally know (or think they know) what their property is worth, and if they're aware that the property is going to be redeveloped for medium-density housing, for example, they will expect the price to reflect that.

As I have already mentioned, you determine the residual land value of the property you want to purchase based on what you think you can achieve as the highest and best use for the land. This does not mean the bulkiest development, but rather the most profitable one that will be well received by the target market and all other stakeholders.

Obtain a sales report for the area that you are looking to purchase in. RealEstate.com and RP Data, for example, offer good reports of all sales made during the previous twelve months categorised into Houses and Home Units by postcode. These reports are valuable because they provide two important pieces of information: the approximate value of the house you want to purchase and (if you study unit sales) the approximate end values of your project once completed. This will help you determine the residual value of the site once you undertake the Feasibility. Remember, the price you agree to pay wants to be somewhere between the market value at the low end and the residual land value at the high end. Once you exceed the RLV, you will of course reduce your profits and increase your risks. Conversely, the closer you are to the market value, the more the profit margin shown in your Feasibility will increase.

Option fee

Regardless of what you may have heard, there is no standard option fee. It may be as low as a token consideration of, say, $1.00 to make the deed of option legal; in my past agreements I have found it somewhere between 0.5% and 0.75%. Generally, I would not pay more than that as an option fee and I would always make it part of the purchase price on settlement.

It is better to have a low option fee as it reduces your risk considerably. For example, if your DA is refused, you are limiting your losses, even if it means paying slightly more for the site, as long as you can justify it through your Feasibility.

Once you have offered the landowner their dream price for their property, their priority is for you to honour the purchase and exercise the option. What I have found is that if I explain to the owner that I want to keep the option fee as low as possible and spend the money instead on making sure I get the DA so I can settle, they are amenable. I have their buy-in.

Option period

When you're negotiating an option, bear in mind that the longer the option period, the more valuable it is for a number of reasons, including the fact that the risk is reduced. The DA can be obtained before the option period runs out, therefore making the site easier to sell. It also provides, if necessary, for the time required to take a matter through the Land and Environment Court (LEC) or its equivalent, depending on where you are.

If you are going to sell the option agreement, provided you have included this in your terms and conditions, the buyer will want to have the maximum period of time to maximise their ability to add value and increase notional equity without the burden of holding costs. In turn, your 'early harvest' – the fee you will take for putting the deal together – will be maximised. Note, by the way, that you need to include the fee you intend to claim in your Feasibility as part of the land acquisition costs, so the buyer of the option does not have to take this out of their profits.

All three items – purchase price, option fee and option period – should be negotiated simultaneously to give you the best overall agreement to suit the situation. So, for example, a longer option period may mean a slightly increased purchase price; a large option fee may mean a slightly reduced purchase price; and so on.

Terms and conditions

The terms and conditions you negotiate will depend on the property you want to acquire and the unique set of circumstances that exist between you and the landowner. However, there are a number of Ts and Cs that must be included in any option agreement where you're intending to redevelop or you risk making the option worthless.

First, the parties to the option must be identified. Always include with your entity the words 'and/or its nominee'. This is critical if you intend to change the name of your entity to your development company, for instance, so you don't pay double stamp duty. More importantly, it allows you to sell the option to someone else. Ideally you will have been following the site to order strategy outlined in Chapter 3, and you will have a buyer ready and waiting to buy the option from you even before the ink is dry.

Second, the owner must consent to allow you, and by default your nominee, to lodge a development application with the council. The terms must also provide that you and your consultants will have access to the property for the purposes of preparing the DA application.

Once you have secured the site you can move on to the next step, which is obtaining approval to develop, thereby creating additional or notional equity. You're on your way.

Chapter 8

DANCE OF THE SEVEN VEILS

Joint ventures

One of the most effective ways to minimise risk, for novice and experienced developers alike, is to enter into a joint venture. In a standard joint venture, each party may invest equally, for example, in a 50/50% share of the required seed capital, with the profits shared equally at the end.

However, there are many ways to undertake a joint venture. I would now like to review a few examples of how a developer can use a joint venture to achieve mutual benefit for all parties.

JVs with landowners

One of the commonest ways to undertake a development is to enter into a joint venture agreement with the owner of the land you want to acquire. Once you have used the Development Site Sourcing Funnel™ method described in Chapter 3 to identify a suitable site, you may wish to propose a JV to the owner as an incentive for them to provide their property for development, basically offering them a share in the profits of the development. Does it mean less profit for the developer? Yes it does. It also means less risk, and that the landowner may be more inclined to come to the party.

To safeguard both the developer and the landowner, it is most important with any joint venture agreement that an appropriate legal structure is used and a formal legal agreement is entered into. Legal structures are discussed further later in the book.

The agreement will often specify that the developer provides no monetary consideration but instead provides the expertise to undertake the development, and the owner puts in his land as equity. The developer organises development finance, obtains the necessary approvals and manages the construction and marketing of the project. In return, the owner receives the agreed value of the land and an agreed share of the profit – say, 60/40 in the owner's favour. The owner in this scenario is often referred to as the Armchair Developer.

Syndicates

Quite often a developer will put together a syndicate of private investors to fund a project. This can be one of the more complex arrangements and can lead to all sorts of complications unless executed properly. Issues that may need to be addressed include:

- Are the members passive investors or will they be actively involved in the day-to-day running of the project?

- Are all the members contributing the same amount of equity?

- How will the profits be distributed?

- Will the members have limited liability or take on full development risks with the developer?

- If a unit trust is utilised, will any of the members want to be a director of the trustee company?

- Are the members' contributions made by way of debt or equity? This is critical when procuring finance from the bank

- How many members will there be in the syndicate?

- Are the members considered to be sophisticated investors?

When putting together this type of structure, or indeed any property development structure, seek the advice of both a solicitor and an accountant specialising in property development. However, in most cases that I have been involved in, a unit trust has been utilised. The unit trust structure is discussed in Chapter 12.

In the unit trust model, the trust deed provides for the administration of the unit trust by the trustee, in this case a trustee company. The solicitor will also create a Unit Holders Agreement, which essentially outlines the agreement between the parties, the amount of investment, their unit entitlements, return on investment and so forth. The challenge with this type of arrangement is that gaining final agreement is often a lengthy process, particularly if there are many members and each seeks the independent advice of their solicitor and accountant. So if there are six syndicate members, plus their partners and advisers, you suddenly have twenty-odd people potentially involved in the decision-making process.

Investor proposals

It is important as the developer that you have a clear outline of your investment proposal. In working through many of these unit holder agreements in the past, my solicitor has compared them to Mata Hari's *Dance of the Seven Veils*. So the negotiations are not protracted, he recommends that everything be divulged to the investors clearly and succinctly upfront but that only limited negotiations be permitted, including on the amount of investment and the date it's required by, the expected ROI and the expected profit distribution time frame.

As a developer, you have to be investor-ready at all times. An investor proposal would normally include:

- Executive summary of the project
- Project overview
- Developer/development team background
- Project legal structure
- Marketing report
- Financial feasibility summary
- Funding summary/model
- Investment sought/investor returns
- Risk analysis
- Time frames.

Appendices:

- Approvals
- Valuations
- Quantity surveyor's construction costs report
- Photo montages.

Always base the amount of investment you seek on what is required and take into account costs of funds and the corresponding effect on project profits. Remember that investor funds are generally more expensive than any other sources of funds and should therefore be utilised only after careful consideration and if supported by the level of profit in the project overall.

Chapter 9

HOW TO GET YOUR APPROVAL - *FAST*

The development approval process

Obtaining the development approval or permit is one of the most important milestones that you will achieve in the property development process. Without a DA nothing will happen. You will not be able to get your funding, buy the land or build your development. Obtaining your DA is also how you achieve *notional equity*, which we will talk about in greater detail in Chapter 13 on funding.

It is absolutely critical therefore that you approach your DA submission with care and a great deal of knowledge about the council and state government instruments that will be used to assess your application. I have seen many development companies go broke because they have gone head to head with the local residents and council in an effort to force through development applications that are often arrogant, or at the very least insensitive to the neighbourhood character and the interests of the residents.

Select an architect who is not only familiar with the type of development you are trying to achieve, but also with your location and the local council. If your architect has a good professional relationship with the council staff, it will be much easier for him or her to negotiate a favourable outcome on your behalf.

Similarly, when selecting your town planner (and the architect will help you with recommendations here), make sure the planner is absolutely knowledgeable about the council, its staff and the locality in general. Often the planner will have previously assessed DAs at the local council, and this will prove to be invaluable when they draft their Statement of Environmental Effects (SEE) in support of your application.

I recommend you visit the council where you are lodging your DA and ask to have a look at some past DAs that are similar to yours and have been approved, or refused for that matter. Review particularly the planner's SEE or impact statement. It will provide you with a wealth of information about what you can expect when you lodge, including previous objections from neighbours.

Unfortunately, the DA process in Australia is still rather cumbersome. However, the good news is that over the past several years the state governments have made an effort to revamp planning legislation and introduce reforms relating to plan preparation, assessment and determination of development proposals. These have included in NSW, for example:

- A completely revamped legislative framework
- Expansion of powers of approval to the Minister
- Creation of the Planning Assessment Commission (PAC)
- Joint Regional Planning Panels (JRPP).

There has also been a trend towards the expansion of what constitutes exempt and complying development. You can find specific information about these on your local council's website.

Generally speaking, councils are seen as overly bureaucratic, inefficient, indecisive and sometimes inconsistent in their decision making. However, current reforms initiated by state governments promise some major improvements and efficiencies in councils' processes for dealing with DAs. In NSW these include, for example, the amalgamation of smaller councils into fewer, more efficient ones.

Having said that, 'blaming' councils or the state government is certainly not what I advocate. Remember, full responsibility and accountability rests with the developer. We have to work with the council to achieve the best outcomes. I recommend adopting an 'issues-based' approach in dealing with the council. That is, remain calm and unemotional at all times, no matter how hairy your application process gets. Identify the issues and prioritise from the most to the least important in relation to the viability of the project. Identify those issues that you are prepared to compromise on as opposed to those that are absolutely critical to the success and profitability of the project, and work with the assessor to resolve differences. Yes, be ready to compromise in order to keep moving forward. Always keep your eyes on the bigger picture.

Here's a snapshot of the development assessment process:

- Concept development
- Pre-lodgement meeting
- Lodgement of the application
- Referrals/notification
- Assessment
- Determination

- Obtaining a Construction Certificate (if DA is approved)

- Construction phase.

Concept development

This is where your due diligence becomes critical. Some pitfalls to avoid are:

- Not assessing the constraints and opportunities of the site before detailing the plans (refer to Chapter 4 on site analysis)

- Not reading or understanding the planning controls and/or planning instruments properly

- Not stress testing your ideas with the consent authority

- Not listening to the feedback from the consent authority

- Pushing the envelope too far.

Pre-lodgement

The pre-lodgement consultation process is very important and can significantly help reduce costs and time taken for a determination. Check with your local council on their pre-lodgement policy, as they tend to vary from council to council. Generally speaking, for a small fee (hundreds as opposed to thousands of dollars) you can book in for a meeting.

This, in my opinion, is an invaluable part of the process and can reveal a great deal about council staff, their appetite for your development and issues you may not be aware of that will affect your submission. I recently went through two pre-lodgement meetings for one of my residential developments (130 apartments), and as a result secured development approval in five months. This included a JRPP (Joint Regional Planning Panel) process, as the state government was the consent authority. I can tell you that gaining approval in just five months in Sydney for this size and complexity of development is an excellent outcome.

Lodgement of the development application

Make sure you fully understand the DA process and the path the application will take within the council and other authorities who will have a say on whether your submission will get approval.

Here are some helpful ideas on how to get it right first time:

Ensure that the application form is completed correctly. Submit all the information requested, and if necessary the correct number of copies of plans. This may not apply if you are able to make an electronic lodgement. You will reduce delays if you lodge a well-prepared and complete application.

If you had a **pre-lodgement meeting**, you would have received written feedback from the council. Make sure all matters raised at pre-lodgement are addressed in the application.

Make sure your town planner provides a thorough **Statement of Environmental Effects**. This is your 'business case' for getting approval: it has to be technically sound and to address issues on merit as necessary. The SEE is defined (by the council) as:

> *...a written statement which demonstrates that the applicant has considered the impact of the proposed development on both the natural and built environments before and after construction and the proposed method/s to mitigate any adverse impact/s...*

Its function is to assist in the assessment of an application.

SEEs are often accompanied by specific information and independent reports from other consultants, depending on the issues being addressed. Common examples include:

- Photomontages
- Examples of public art
- Acoustic report
- Traffic report
- Environmental report.

Referrals

The council has a statutory obligation under the EP&A Act to refer DA applications to other statutory authorities for their consideration if the proposed scheme will affect their jurisdiction. They may also seek expert assessment on specific issues as required. Common referrals include:

- Heritage
- Fire department
- Roads and maritime services
- Airport authority.

This means you may have to provide specialist documentation with your application.

Notification

Similarly, the council has a statutory obligation to notify the immediate neighbours and the public that a development application is being considered. This is generally done by way of advertising in the local paper, on the council's website and by letter directly to the neighbours.

Assessment

The council is legally obligated to assess the application with reference to the applicable provisions, and there are many. Here are some of the relevant instruments:

- Environmental Planning and Assessment Act (EP&A Act)

- State Environmental Planning Policies (SEPP)

- Regional Environmental Planning Policies (REPP)

- Environmental Planning Instruments (e.g. IDOs, PSOs, LEPs)

- Development Control Plans and Council Policies (DCPs).

It is important to remember that councils are scrutinised not only on their decisions, but on their processes in coming to those decisions – that is, they have to follow due process.

This is particularly relevant in dealing with objections from adjoining neighbours, which is where you have to help the council to help you. Take into consideration the neighbours' issues and address them accordingly. This will help the council deal with potential objections if and when they receive them.

Determination

The council's options for determination are set out under the EP&A Act:

Approval. Your approval will come with conditions of consent. You must ensure that you read your approval completely as it often contains actions required on your part. There are also critical dates that need to be adhered to, including the expiry date of the DA if no action is taken. This is often only two years, although there is a short grace period during which you can reinstate. Nevertheless, I have come across situations where the applicant has inadvertently allowed their DA to lapse and has had to reapply for a completely new DA. Worse still, sometimes the planning densities have changed for the worse, which means the applicant suffers a great lost opportunity. Remember, once the DA has lapsed, the council does not have the power to reinstate.

Refusal. If your application is refused, you do have some avenues for appeal and/or review under the EP&A Act. The Notice of Refusal from the council will set out your rights for appeal. Generally speaking, you can have the decision reviewed by independent staff within the council, which is the quickest and cheapest option. Alternatively, you can lodge an appeal at the Land and Environment Court as it is commonly known (although it has changed its name to NCAT in NSW and VCAT in Victoria).

Deferred Commencement. If you receive an approval with Deferred Commencement as one of the conditions of consent, it means that certain actions have to be completed and evidenced to the council before you can activate your DA. Those actions will be clearly stated in your conditions of consent.

More than 90% of all applications are determined under delegated authority (that is, by council staff rather than going to a meeting for councillors to decide). It is therefore worthwhile to determine from your council the criteria for getting approval under delegated authority, as it is quicker and less complex than to have your application referred to councillors and perhaps encounter some political risks.

Construction Certificate (Building) Approval

Construction Certificate Approval is required before construction can commence. Be aware of conditions imposed in the development consent.

Additional information and actions will be required, and fees, including developer contributions, will need to be paid before the Construction Certificate can be issued.

Summary

The planning process is challenging. Understanding the process well and approaching it in an issues-based way will assist you greatly. Here's a quick summary of the pitfalls to avoid and the main points we have covered.

Pitfalls include:

- Poor research
- Poor preparation and PR work prior to lodgement
- Lack of communication with the consent authority (ask the right questions)
- Failure to understand the importance of threshold issues (height, FSR, setbacks, car parking, views, contamination, etc.)

- Incomplete or poor information
- Poor understanding of the political process
- Failure to anticipate potential problems.

Successful applicants:

- Understand the process
- Do their homework
- Resource and prepare their proposal well
- Communicate effectively and *at appropriate times* in the process
- Problem solve effectively
- Demonstrate reasonableness at all times
- Understand the threshold issues
- Concede where necessary
- Keep the final goal in sight.

Other matters:

- Likely impact of the development (on both natural and built environments)
- Suitability of the site for the development
- Any submissions (objections) received
- The public interest.

How and where to find assistance

- Council's website

- Austlii

- Department of Planning website

- Local Environmental Plans (LEPs), Development Control Plans (DCPs)

- Building Code of Australia (BCA), Australian Standards (AS) and relevant guidelines.

Chapter 10

PROPERTY DEVELOPMENT IS A TEAM SPORT

Choosing your team: the role of consultants

Having the right team around you will almost certainly be one of the most critical success factors for your development. Indeed it may be decisive in whether the bank approves your development loan and your ability to attract private investors.

It is doubly critical if you are just starting out and you lack the experience to reassure the bank that you can pull it off.

Remember, when the bank looks at your application, they scrutinise two things. One is the financial feasibility and robustness of the project itself – in another words, does it 'stack up' and is there enough development margin or profit in it? The other object of scrutiny is you, the developer. Do you have the ability to complete the project? And if you do not have the experience, then you can add weight to your case by appointing experienced consultants, in particular a good and reputable project manager.

The process for selecting your consultants is absolutely crucial. I took on my first project, *La Vie en Rose*, some eighteen years ago. During my interview on applying for a development loan from the bank, I was told by the manager that though he believed the project was financially sound, because I had never tackled a property development project before I would have to hire an experienced project manager for the duration of the project. He actually referred me to a project management company that will remain nameless.

So, as you'll recall, the next day I turned up at the company's city office in Sydney and announced enthusiastically to all and sundry, 'Hi there. The bank sent me. I'm looking for a project manager!'

What's wrong with this picture? Well, as I was to find out later, despite the referral from my financier being well-meant, this is *not* how you select your consultants. Why not? After all, the bank would not give you a bum steer to have you fail. It wouldn't make sense. As a stakeholder, they would surely want you to succeed, and pay back the loan and interest – wouldn't they?

Well, yes, but bankers are not developers. As is the case with the myriad of consultants you will deal with, they will offer you advice in good faith. However, it is *always* your responsibility to verify the information you receive, checking and double checking it regardless of who is offering it.

My first project manager was instrumental in the selection of a builder who was overpriced and dishonest, and who eventually went bankrupt during the project. Indeed, as recounted in Chapter 6, he nearly dragged me into bank-ruptcy with him. I did not escape unscathed, though, and it cost me all my profit, but I survived and got out by the skin of my teeth.

That's the sort of damage that one consultant, albeit one of the most important ones, can inflict on your project. I am currently about to lodge a development application for an eleven-storey mixed commercial, retail and residential development, with one- and two-bedroom apartments, in inner-city Sydney.

Here's the list of consultants I have to engage just to lodge the DA.

Architect

Town planner

Landscape architect

Quantity surveyor

Land surveyor

Heritage consultant

Acoustic consultant

Structural engineer

Geotechnical engineer

Contamination consultant

Hydraulic engineer

Traffic consultant

BCA consultant

Access consultant

Reflectivity consultant

Waste management consultant

Environment management consultant

Thermal consultant

Model maker and architectural images consultant

I may also require:

Archaeological baseline report

Plan of management

Security management plan

Wind effects report

Critical habitat species impact statement

So what's the best way to set up your project and select the most competent consultants to support you in your venture? Well, the first thing I do is create my Organisation Chart .

Organisation Chart

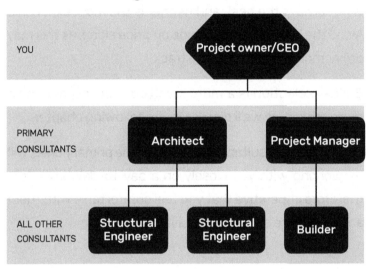

Of course, this is not a strict hierarchy. There will be direct interaction between the CEO and other consultants, including the builder, between the architect and the project manager, and so forth.

What the diagram conveys is that the architect is responsible for the performance of the consultants, and indeed will often recommend consultants to the CEO. However, the CEO should be involved first hand in the selection of *all* the consultants and establish a clear selection process. I would recommend that you invite at least three consultants from each discipline to submit their fee proposal for consideration. Carry out reference checks with previous developers, financiers, quantity surveyors and accountants before final selection. Remember that the cheapest is not always the best, and neither is the most expensive. Avoid the temptation to decide on price alone, as this may prove more costly down the track.

Builder selection is a more involved process, and even more critical, as we'll discuss in the following chapter.

Finally, your consultants, particularly the primary ones, will be working with you closely on a day-to-day basis. It is therefore imperative that you feel comfortable with them and that there are no personality clashes.

Chapter 11

FINDING BOB

Tendering for the builder

Tendering for the builder has to be handled with care and discipline if you're to find the right contractor at the right price.

What is a tender? In construction, the main tender process is generally for the selection of the contractor who will construct the works. It involves a submission in response to an invitation to tender an offer to perform work at a given price.

Successful tendering will depend on a number of things, including:

- Documentation
- Quality of building contractors
- State of the market
- Management of the tender process.

Documentation. The quality of your documentation, which typically includes architectural, engineering and other relevant consultants' plans and specifications, will determine the quality and accuracy of the responses from building contractors.

In order for the submissions to reflect the same build outcome, the documentation must be detailed and unambiguous. For larger projects it is usually accompanied by a Bill of Quantities from the quantity surveyor. An experienced architect and/or project manager will ensure coordination of all of the consultants' documentation.

Of course, the tenderers will differ on their price and the time they will take to finish the job, which is where the negotiations become critical.

Quality of building contractors. However good your documentation is, unless the quality of building contractors on your tender list is of a high standard and correctly matched to the type of construction work you want, you will not succeed in getting the right contractor. You have to fish in the right pond.

An experienced architect would have curated over a number of years a list of building contractors they are comfortable in recommending, as would an experienced project manager. Another excellent source of information regarding the performance of builders (remember, sometimes they're only as good as their last job) is the quantity surveyor.

A quantity surveyor who works with builders every day, assessing their work and recommending progress payments to the developer and the bank, can provide great insight into how efficient the builder is, whether they're performing on time and on budget, and indeed whether they are difficult or easy to work with. Never underestimate the negative effect a personality clash between you and the building contractor will have on your project. Always make sure you're comfortable working with them for the twelve to eighteen months it might take to complete your project.

State of the market. A builder who is not hungry enough for the work will charge you a high price. Builders often get hungry as opposed to desperate because they're finishing a project and want to avoid downtime between jobs. They may be trying to grow their business in a new market or they simply find your project attractive because of its location, the type of construction or they see it as a catalyst for other similar work.

If there is a general downturn in the industry, building contractors, as well as the sub-trades, will be much more competitive in their pricing in order to secure projects. Take care, however, to ensure the contractor is financially sound and not taking too much risk in their pricing. There is then the risk that they will try to claw back profits they have forgone to win the job through variations during the works. There must always be the right balance between the builder's profit margin and their enthusiasm to win a tender.

Managing the tender process. Good execution of the tender process will save time and money and ensure that the right building contractor wins the job. It is critical to have a quantity surveyor on board to help manage the process, together with your architect and project manager.

Figure 11.1 illustrates the main elements of the typical tendering process.

The goal of the tendering process is not necessarily to obtain the cheapest possible price for a project, but rather to minimise project risks by appointing a contractor who will deliver to the predetermined scope and quality, within the time frame and budget derived from the developer's feasibility analysis.

Figure 11.1. Tender Process

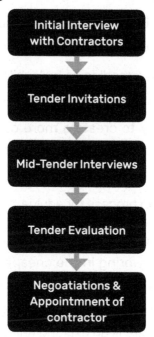

Negotiated contract

An alternative to the competitive tender is the nego-tiated contract. The process involves you and/or your consultants – namely, your project manager, your quan-tity surveyor (armed with a Bill of Quantities), and your architect - negotiating with a preferred builder for a price, rather than calling for tenders.

Advantages to this approach include:

- ▪ More accurate pricing
- ▪ More thorough assessment of the builder's capacity, both financially and operationally

- Time saved in contracting the builder
- Greater certainty of the builder's ability to complete the project on time and within budget
- Better understanding of buildability issues and the opportunity to alleviate potential variations
- Opportunity to create a more collaborative spirit and better working relationship with the builder.

Often, too, it may be possible to bring the builder on board early in the design process for advice.

However, with no competition from other builders, this method will rarely bring in the cheapest price. Furthermore, there needs to be a level of trust between the parties to make this work. I would suggest trying this method only if there is an existing relationship from past projects, if not between the developer and the builder, then at least between the architect and the builder.

Managing the construction process

The construction phase of your project is a major milestone in your 7-Phase Property Development Process. By the time construction starts you will have sourced a development site, procured funding, negotiated acquisition (preferably through a call option), completed the design development process, drawn up architectural plans and supporting documents, lodged the development (DA) application, possibly contended with neighbours and/or the council, gained approval, obtained the construction certificate (CC), tendered for a building contractor and undertaken the necessary pre-sales to satisfy your bank's lending criteria so you can access your funds. You're now ready to see the fruits of your labour and vision take shape.

Like the other phases of the development process, the construction phase needs to be managed utilising the skills of your two primary consultants – the project manager, whom you will also appoint as contract administrator, and the architect. The quantity surveyor also plays a key role in acting for the bank and assisting in cost management. The respective roles of these key consultants were outlined in Chapter 10.

The key risk factors during the construction phase typically include (but are not restricted to):

- Selection and performance of the project manager
- Selection and performance of the building contractor
- Costs overruns (as a result of variations)
- Delays in construction
- Exceeding construction budget
- Losing off-plan sales because of delays beyond sunset clauses
- Being sued under the Security of Payments Act
- Disputes.

I am assuming that the builder has been contracted under a lump-sum fixed term contract, which is most often a bank requirement for lending for construction. The builder is therefore responsible for all of his subcontractors. You, as developer, are responsible for the selection and performance of the project manager, who in turn is responsible for managing all of the risks listed above and any others arising during construction.

Chapter 12

PROTECTING YOUR ASSETS

Structures for property development and other legal issues

When it comes to structuring my property development business and projects, I always seek the best advice from my lawyer and accountant, and I urge you to do the same. This phase of the property development process is critical to establishing your business correctly and will have a huge impact on your funding, your investors, protection of your assets, limiting your risks and liabilities, and of course the tax efficiency of your scheme.

In considering the structure, you need to discuss the pros and cons of the following types of entities:

- Partnerships
- Joint ventures
- Companies
- Unit trusts
- Discretionary trusts.

After careful consideration, you and your adviser may well decide to combine the positive attributes of two or more of the above entities to give you the best result.

I am not qualified or licensed to provide tax advice. However, I will flag a number of issues that you might like to consider and discuss with your advisers when choosing your structure *before* acquiring property for redevelopment. I refer here primarily to mixed-use (commercial and residential) and purely residential developments.

The main issues revolve around:

- GST on acquisition, construction and sale
- Capital gains
- Interest deductibility
- Determining which structure will maximise the tax efficiency of your scheme
- Determining whether your structure meets your financier's requirements

- Determining whether your structure attracts investors by maximising their benefits.

While you should not expect to pay no tax, ideally your advisers will counsel you on how to reduce your overall level of taxation, offset losses, claim deductions on interest and extract profit from your structure without incurring additional tax.

Significantly, if you have private investors, they will require their own independent advice on how to amalgamate their personal structure with yours for their maximum benefit. Your structure has to be 'investor friendly', otherwise you may not be able to secure their funds.

As I mentioned in an earlier chapter, consider your exit strategies in the planning stage of your business. I often hear would-be developers say, 'Oh, I'm going to develop six town houses and I'll probably keep a couple.' They do not realise the implications their intention may have on their structure and their tax position. Your adviser will tell you that if you are doing property development in the true sense – that is, you are developing and then on-selling within the shortest time possible – your profits will be accounted for as revenue, but if you are developing and then holding as an investment, your profits will be accounted for as capital gains.

When considering the most appropriate structure, it is important to remember you will discuss with your adviser both the tax implications and the commercial aspects of your business. Your chosen entity should not only provide an improvement of your overall tax position but should also enable you to:

- Protect your assets from external claims
- Adjust income and capital entitlements
- Introduce new equity (as opposed to debt) participants
- Meet the bank's lending criteria.

My preferred structure

Over the years I have experimented with many structures and, more often than not, I now use a unit trust because it fits my business model of being able to use multiple sources of funds for development. Figure 12.1 shows what it looks like.

Figure: 12.1. Structure of a unit trust

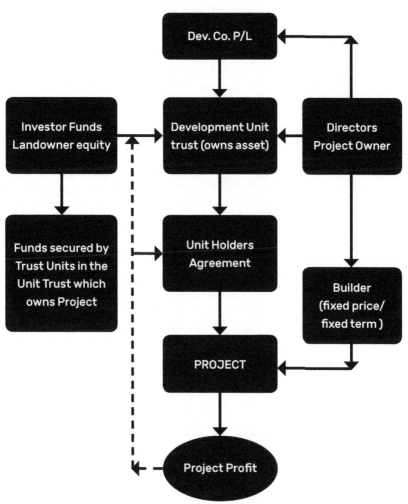

Chapter 13

SHOW ME THE MONEY

Property development finance

Contrary to popular belief, property development is not all about building and construction. It is mostly about funding and managing the budget before and during construction. Indeed, the main reason for failure in property development is lack or mismanagement of funds.

Property development finance is unique. It is absolutely crucial that you, as CEO of a property development business, learn how to determine correctly the source and application of funds for your project.

Here I'll begin by outlining the basics of property development finance before demonstrating some fundamentals to making sure your project is fundable by the cheapest source of this finance: the bank.

As already noted, before providing finance, the bank will look at two components of the deal: the financial feasibility of your project (whether it 'stacks up') and your experience as a developer. I will discuss these two components in detail later in this chapter.

Basically, there are two types of funding: equity and debt. Further, there are two types of equity: actual equity and notional equity, and two types of debt: first mortgage or senior debt and mezzanine debt.

You may utilise a combination of funding sources, as illustrated below. It's important when deciding the best funding structure that you also determine the costs of funds and how those costs will affect your financial feasibility.

Funding Pyramid

Initial equity

Notional equity

Mezzanine debt (2nd mortgage)

Senior debt (first mortgage)

Funding structure

Initial equity. Initial equity is that part of the purchase and development cost that is not provided by the first mortgage provider. It can be viewed by the first mortgagee as the developer's 'hurt money'. It can be borrowed from another source against other security, and indeed could be made up using mezzanine finance, although this is not recommended as it is a costly form of finance and increases project risk significantly.

The Bank will insist that your initial equity is used first before you will have access to the bank funds.

Notional equity. Notional equity is the gold nugget that's hidden in every good property development deal. You can create notional equity in many different ways, and indeed you can create so much of it that often you don't need to inject any money into the deal.

Some of the ways that notional equity can be achieved are rezoning of the site, adding value by obtaining a DA for redevelopment, removing easements and strata titling an existing building. Asset value can also increase when a move in asset prices occurs over a period of time (for example, in cases where delayed settlement terms have been agreed), or simply when the first mortgage lender recognises increased value (on-completion valuation).

Mezzanine debt. Mezzanine debt sits *behind* the senior or first mortgage debt. It is therefore subordinate to the first mortgage, and usually requires second mortgage security as well as directors' guarantees.

However, it sits *before* owner's equity and can be a combination of both debt and equity. It has a predetermined income yield and is sometimes referred to as seed capital.

Utilising mezzanine finance for property development is not recommended as it can be expensive, both to establish the loan and because it commands high interest rates. The terms and conditions are also often very stringent. While there is a place for mezzanine funds in some circumstances, this finance is generally to be avoided. If your feasibility analysis is such that it requires mezzanine finance, I would recommend finding another project with less risk.

Senior debt. The senior debt, or first mortgage, will be financed through your principal lender. Assuming that lender is a bank, for example, it will take first mortgage security over all assets in the deal and it will require directors' guarantees. Currently the terms and conditions for lending typically include the following (bear in mind, however, that these are constantly changing based on market conditions and the bank's policies, so determine the latest criteria when you are ready to borrow or when doing feasibility studies.

Financial modelling and funding

Once you have completed your financial feasibility, the next steps are to build the following:

- A funding table showing that the deal meets lending criteria and is fundable by the bank and/ or other preferred sources of funds

- A source and application table demonstrating the source of those funds, how they will be utilised through the project, the return of seed capital and the distribution of profits

- An investor and cost of funds model

- Sensitivity models showing the effects on profit, loan to value ratios (LVR) and funding

- A cash flow forecast.

Your funding model should allow you to determine the best funding structure for your project and whether it will be fundable by the bank, while at the same time allowing you to maximise notional equity and provide you and your investors, if there are any, with maximum returns.

Development funding submissions. Typically, the following information is required when preparing a submission for funding:

- Detailed feasibilities indicating all the costings estimated to complete the project, including council contributions, professional fees, project manager, demolition

- Details of leases or potential leases (if applicable)
- Copy of tenancy schedule (if applicable)
- Copy of valuation (if available)
- Copy of quantity surveyor's report (if available)
- CV of borrowers/guarantors (brief only)
- CV of builder (if available) or list of past projects if owner-builder
- Details of facility required
- Copies of the business's last two years' financial statements (balance sheet, profit and loss statements) for all related **company** and/or **trust** accounts
- Copies of last two years' tax returns for any **director, partner** or **guarantor** related to the application
- Statement of assets and liabilities for each borrower/guarantor
- Contract of sale (if purchasing property)
- Details of any other loans and/or credit facilities, including hire purchase and leasing (e.g. balance, term remaining, repayments, residual/balloon)
- Trust deeds, including the names, addresses and ages of all beneficiaries
- Diagram showing the borrowing entity and any other related entities, if applicable (including trusts, companies, etc.)

- Copy of lease profile for each asset detailing income, expenses, lease start date, lease completion date, options and non-recoverable expenses.

Here are the top tips from one of the big four banks to avoid common errors in submissions for (senior debt) development funding:

- A project **funding table** must be prepared and should include all project development costs (other than selling costs, which are payable at settlement)

- Where the project is being sold upon completion, **GST on development costs** should be excluded from the funding table. GST is to be separately funded by the borrower or via an overdraft account, which is self-liquidating and then cleared by input tax credits

- If the development site has been recently purchased, the **land value** in the project funding table should be the lower of cost and valuation. If the site has been held for some time (twelve months or more), unless it has been enhanced with a development approval and land value is adopted in lieu of cost, the acquisition costs should *not* be included in the funding table. When you're using an 'as is' valuation that assumes the payment of fees/costs (e.g. council contributions), these fees/costs should *not* be separately shown in the funding table in order to prevent (a) double-counting and (b) overstating equity

- Where the quantity surveyor's estimate of **construction costs** exceeds the borrower's estimate and/or the building contract, it is the QS's estimate that should be used in the funding table

- One hundred per cent of **equity** must be contributed upfront, prior to any debt funding. This is to ensure that once debt funding commences, the bank holds sufficient approved funds to complete the project (including a minimum 5% contingency allowance within the facility limit)

- The proposed **facility amount** must reconcile to total debt required per the funding table

- The **security value** is the total project development cost (per the funding table), *not* the 'as if complete' value. The 'as if complete' value is used only to confirm the development project's viability

- A **project feasibility** must be prepared, calculating the margin between the 'as if complete' value (net of selling costs and GST) and the total project cost (per the funding table). This margin as a percentage of total project cost is termed the return on cost

- **GST** on both **gross realisations** (if residential) and **selling costs** must be included in the project feasibility, even when the property is to be retained on completion (in order to determine the theoretical development profit/project viability). As selling costs are a settlement adjustment, they should *not* be included in the funding table (unless incurred upfront in relation to pre-sales)

- A **return on cost** below market expectations of 17–20% may indicate that (a) the adopted land value is overstated and (b) the gearing is understated

- A **borrower's CV** and **builder's CV** are to be provided, as the bank needs to understand the borrower's and builder's experience

- **Serviceability** pre- and post-sales is to be completed so the bank can understand the debt levels the client has the capacity to service should they be seeking less than policy on pre-sales – 100% debt cover

- **Statements of assets and liabilities** and financial accounts are to be provided and cannot be mitigated by pre-sales.

Chapter 14

HOW THE BANK ASSESSES YOUR FUNDING SUBMISSION

It is important to have a pre-submission meeting with your bank representative and to understand the bank's assessment criteria. Here are one of the top four banks' internal guidelines for assessing development finance. Not all of the information provided here will be applicable to every funding submission, but you can use this as a guide to see whether you meet the bank's criteria before committing to a particular project. It will provide you with a basis for discussion with your chosen bank. Here's what the bank will be looking for:

Purpose. A statement of purpose for each credit facility should say what the funds are expected to be used for *and* what has caused your underlying need to obtain financing. Your stated use for a loan may not be the whole story. The bank will want to understand the true borrowing cause so that it can provide the solution that best meets your needs and that of the bank.

History. This includes:

- Basic past account history, including background to relationship, risk of loss to other banks, industry background, recent large projects and any other relevant customer background information
- Background purpose/borrowing cause of existing facilities.

The following details will be required by the bank:

Borrower/customer group:

- Corporate structure
- Length of customer relationship.

Type of transaction:

- Property development.

Type of property:

- Office
- Retail
- Industrial
- Leisure/hospitality
- Residential development
- Other (please specify).

Property/project details:

- Type (see above)
- Size/area/number of units
- Total development cost/budget
- Time to complete project
- Sales value (on completion)
- Rental income and tenancy details if appropriate (break down into pre-committed and speculative).

Property/project cost:

- Cost of development, broken into component parts including land and acquisition costs, development/ consultants' costs, construction costs, finance costs, marketing costs and project contingency
- Include a copy of the development appraisal and cash flow with the credit application.

Use of funds:

- What are the funds being used for?
- How is the transaction being financed?
- Include funding table showing:
  - Total development cost
  - Equity/borrower stake
  - Debt (bank and other third-party borrowings)
  - Equity + debt = cost of development
  - Show relative percentages – debt/equity.

Funding must be on a cost to complete basis with all equity injected into the development ahead of bank debt.

Loan details:

- Amount (loan to cost ratio), term (loan maturity must be after anticipated completion date).

Repayment source:

- Sale of property upon completion
- Summarise sale expectations for the property/ project and anticipated completion timetable.

Compliance:

- Compliance with policy – Any non-compliance issues for both existing and new facilities proposed will be determined

■ Compliance with existing approval conditions or covenants. Determine any breaches.

Debt servicing

Analysis of the debt servicing capacity of the property being developed depends on the anticipated method of repayment of the development loan.

There are two primary means of repayment of a commercial property development loan: sale of the property/development at practical completion and refinance of the development loan by the drawdown of a term loan.

For our purposes, we are referring only to the first point above, where repayment is to be from the sale of the property/development on completion.

Sale of the property/development. Usually interest will be capitalised during the construction/development phase of a property or project. The loan amount, inclusive of interest capitalised, will be repaid on completion through the sale of the property. In such circumstances, the expectation is that the borrower will not need to service the facility post completion.

Debt servicing analysis. The bank undertakes a debt servicing analysis, which is based upon a hypothetical calculation of what the debt servicing position would be if the property did not sell as expected. The primary analysis focuses on the debt servicing position of the borrower. The borrower's debt servicing capacity is determined based either on cash flow or profit.

However, the borrower may not be able to demonstrate debt servicing capacity from its historic financial information. This will often be the case if a special purpose vehicle without trading history is undertaking the development. The ability to service the proposed debt may then depend on rental income from the subject property or on resources or income external to the project (such as guarantors/project sponsors).

Where the ability to service depends on rental income from the property/project, this capacity will be detailed and critically assessed by the bank by considering factors such as:

- The level and strength of any pre-committed leases (if applicable)
- Current market rents for equivalent properties. These will be sensitised to determine the discounts that could be applied while still servicing the proposed debt
- Current market demand conditions and ease of letting (where pre-commitments are not held).

Where the borrower does not have the capacity to service and repay the proposed debt (for example, where 'special purpose' entities are used for the development), there may also be reliance on the resources of guarantors or project sponsors. It would then be appropriate to include further assessment of the financial position of guarantors or project sponsors. In such circumstances, an additional debt servicing table using financial information obtained for the guarantors or sponsors is detailed. The bank will also determine if there is a legally enforceable right of recourse to other parties.

The credit assessor's comments are provided on the following, as applicable:

- Is a deficiency in debt servicing capacity evident?

- Is a material change evident in the historic results or likely during the term of the facility? The assessor will look at changes occurring in historic results (year on year) and between historic results and projections.

Material changes could be either positive or negative. Comment will be made where an item in the debt servicing calculation moves from positive to negative, shows a downward trend (particularly after a number of growth periods), or shows positive or negative changes that are above normal. As a guide, movements in any item greater than 10% (positive or negative) must be considered.

Where historic financial statements can be analysed for the borrower, the assessor will comment on sensitivity analysis in accordance with current policy.

Cash flow forecast

In *all* property development loan applications, cash flow forecasts for the development/construction phase are required.

The borrower should provide the bank with a cash flow forecast for the development and sales phases (sometimes known as the Development Budget or Project Summary). This should outline all cost items required to bring the development to practical completion and when they are expected to be incurred. This will need to be tabled and analysed by the banker.

Cost items to be included in the cash flow forecast include, but are not limited to:

- Land cost
- Land acquisition costs
- Development costs
- Consultants costs
- Planning/permit costs
- Construction costs
- Marketing costs
- Lease incentives
- Finance costs (legal, valuation, etc.)
- Bank interest
- Project contingency.

Assessment will be made of the reasonableness and achievability of the project cash flow forecast/project summary, with particular comment under the following headings:

Development costs budgeted. The credit assessor will assess the project costs budgeted to ensure all appropriate costs are included and that cost estimates are reasonable, given the development type and current market/industry conditions. The assessor will also confirm that adequate allowance has been made for Goods and Services Tax or other equivalent taxes that may affect development costs.

Funding of borrower's equity in project. The assessor will comment on the amount, timing and source of the forecast equity contribution to the project. Equity contributions are made prior to any bank (debt) funding.

Adequacy of debt funding. The assessor will confirm that the level of funding sought is sufficient to complete the project, after the borrower's equity contribution has been made.

Sales revenues projected. The assessor will:

- Comment on the level, timing and source of sales revenue forecast
- Assess assumptions made about current/expected economic and property market conditions

- Consider demand conditions within the project's target market, what levels of pre-sales are forecast, what pre-sales have been achieved to date, what sales prices are expected, what reliance there is on speculative sales, whether these assumptions are reasonable and adequate allowance has been made for taxes that may impact on sale proceeds.

Cash flow forecasts – borrower/guarantor/sponsor

The assessor may also obtain and assess cash flow forecasts for the borrower, guarantor(s) or project sponsor(s) (as appropriate), with specific comment on:

Capacity to make the required equity contributions. Where is the equity contribution being sourced? Are there any factors that could adversely impact on the capacity of the party to make such contributions when required?

Ability to cover potential cost overruns. What capacity exists to cover potential cost overruns or contingencies on the project? Assessment of other resources and income sources of the borrower/guarantor(s)/sponsor(s)

Capacity to service proposed debt facilities. What capacity does (do) the borrower/guarantor(s)/sponsor(s) have to service the proposed facilities in the event of project delays or delays in settling (or failure to complete) sale contracts?

The assessor will comment on the scope/requirement for interest rate hedging. Analysis of cash flow quality flows directly through to exit analysis (as discussed later in this chapter).

Management/management information systems

Management's actions may directly affect the performance of a business and hence the risk of any credit. The impact of management in property development lending is primarily a function of the level of experience of the developer and the level of market/speculative risk in the project. The greater the experience (as evidenced by the developer's track record of successful property development in projects of similar size and nature to the subject project), the less the management risk. The higher the market/speculative risk (as evidenced by factors such as the development of property/space with pre-committed sales or leases), the greater the reliance on management to mitigate the market risks inherent in such a development. The less the market risks (as evidenced by acceptable levels of pre-commitment), the more the developer has demonstrated his or her management expertise and reduced market risk.

This analysis demonstrates the impact management skills and experience might have on changes in cash flow. Assessment of management takes into consideration the following:

- Experience of management (noting any recent management changes)

- Depth of management (considering succession planning and key person insurance)

- Breadth of management in key functional areas

- Integrity of management

- Use of appropriate and independent advisers on an ongoing basis

- Management's track record in achieving successful results and the management information systems used to track them.

Specifically, the credit assessor will want to evaluate and quantify management's historic performance in the following areas:

- Coping with economic/property market downturns

- Maximising the level of pre-commitment (whether leases or sales) prior to the development commencing

- Maximising the level of income from a partly or wholly developed property on a speculative basis

- Achieving the balance between pre-committed and speculative revenues to maximise development profit consistently

- Managing interest rate risk and changes in interest rates

- Delivering projects on time and within budget.

Success in these management areas requires that managers:

- Understand how economic conditions affect the performance of the market/property, anticipate the effects of those conditions and have plans for coping with them

- Understand how competitors are likely to affect the business's/development's performance

- Anticipate and manage the effects of actions by competitors.

The credit assessor will provide comment on the following, as applicable:

- Family tree, noting consolidated/inter-company relationships including ownership of assets and flow of income

- Nature and composition of board and senior management.

Customer rating system and risk profile

The bank's Customer Rating System and Risk Profile identify and quantify an objective view of the customer's financial position by analysis of their current and projected financial statements. The risk score and resultant profile is intended to focus financial analysis on the riskier elements of the borrower's financial statements in a predetermined range of, say, 1–15. Financial risk is concerned with the viability and stability of the customer's repayment sources. By performing a financial statement analysis, the assessor will quantify the company's ability to repay its debt.

A trend analysis of the customer's financial position is undertaken where possible, with brief comments on the results documented. Further in-depth analysis may also be required if the financial risk score exceeds the bank's current minimum threshold. The **liquidity/cash flow risk component** measures the ease with which a customer can meet their short-term cash needs via the cash flows generated by the property. In property development lending, the focus of the analysis should be on the borrower's ability to fund cost overruns occurring during the development/construction phase and the borrower's ability to service interest on the facility post construction.

The **capital structure risk component** measures the relationship between borrowed funds (debt) and company funds (equity). Analysis is based on the cost of the development, not the anticipated end value. It also indicates the extent of financial risk carried by the owners and creditors respectively.

The **market risk component** measures the amount of market risk in a transaction and is a function of the level and quality of pre-commitments (either lease or sale or both) of end users of the property.

Commercial property development lending – specific guidelines

Assessors will also consider the following:

- The borrower's experience/track record in property development in terms of the size and complexity of the development, the proposed market sector and the borrower's success in previous developments
- The level of pre-commitments (leases or sales) relative to debt servicing requirement or debt level
- The quality of cash flow, split between pre-committed and speculative sales and rentals (if appropriate)
- Tenant quality (if appropriate)
- The lease maturity profile (if appropriate).

Property/project risk and competitive position

While the analysis, to this point, has focused on the developer's future projections, it is important for the assessor to compare the project's likely success against peer/comparable (by location and type of property) or competing developments. This will enable a better determination of whether the proposed development is potentially successful or unsuccessful.

To complete this analysis, the assessor uses a group of properties/developments of a similar size and type in a similar location to the subject development to compare their respective merits. In particular, they consider how the characteristics/variables of the subject development (sales prices, location, tenants, cost, property features, etc.) compare with other examples in the market. This analysis is particularly important where a substantial level of market/property risk is inherent in the development (where pre-commitments are not a significant feature of the development).

It is also important to compare pre-commitment variables (sales value per sq. m., rent per sq. m., lease terms, lease incentives, tenant quality, etc.) with those being achieved elsewhere in the market by comparable product.

In using any information for comparative purposes, the bank's assessor will be sensitive to several considerations, including:

The size of the comparative group. If only two comparable properties/developments are included, the resulting average may not be representative of the property type.

The date of the peer group data. If the data is several years old, then a comparison using current data for the subject property may be of little value.

The geographical mixture of the peer group. Comparing the property with others in a geographical region may be more relevant than comparing a cross-section of properties across a state or country.

The quality of the data. How reliable is the data being used and are ratios calculated in the same manner as for the subject property?

The assessor will make comments under each of the following headings, specifically considering market conditions and the property/project's competitive position (with reference to peer comparison, as appropriate):

Property/project risk assessment. The fit of the property/project (that is, the type, quality and price of the project on offer) for that particular location and in comparison with competing properties/developments. Is it the right development, in the right location, at the right price, at the right time?

Professional team. The assessor will detail and assess the make-up and capabilities of the professional team supporting the project, so demonstrate where possible that they have the expertise and track record appropriate for a project of this type and scale.

Developer's experience. Demonstrate to them that you as the developer have the track record/expertise appropriate for a project of this type and scale.

Location/site. How does the property's location compare with competing properties? Are there others in the area competing for the same purchasers and tenants? Is the development appropriate for that location?

Enforceable pre-commitments – pre-sales and pre-leases (if appropriate). The assessor will look at the quantity, quality and spread of pre-sales and pre-leases (if appropriate) *relative to the debt proposed*. Are contracts unconditional, arm's length and enforceable? Are there sunset clauses (for completion) in the contracts? How do prices compare with the market?

For single purchasers, assessors will comment on financial strength and ability to complete the transaction. For multiple purchasers, they will assess the quantity and quality of pre-sales with comments on:

- Level and type of deposits/security bonds
- Diversity of purchasers
- Related party purchasers
- Sales to non-residents
- Sunset dates for completion
- Allowance of sales commissions, taxes, legal costs in contracts.

Demand analysis (uncommitted portion of project). The assessor will analyse existing and future market demand for the portion of the property not subject to pre-sale commitments (keeping the depth of analysis relative to the level of commitments already achieved).

Marketing strategy. They will comment on the marketing strategy the developer is adopting in relation to the uncommitted portion of the project.

Quality of construction/fit-out. How does the property/project compare with competing properties in terms of quality of construction and fit-out? This is particularly important if the development is proceeding on a speculative basis (that is, a low level of pre-committed tenants/purchasers).

Construction and assessment of builder. How complex or simple is the construction? Who is the builder? What is their technical and financial capacity to meet their commitments under the building contract? Is a performance guarantee being obtained or required?

Building contract. The assessor will require an outline of the key features of the contract. Is it fixed term/fixed price? Does it conform to acceptable industry standards? What are the security retention provisions, and do they meet the bank's policy requirements?

Property market and other risks

It is appropriate to consider the broader market risks that could specifically impact on the project/development. These risks may impact on the borrower's ability to repay the development facilities as expected.

The assessor will make comments under each of the following headings. Note that the depth of such analysis will be relative to the level and quality of pre-commitments already achieved at the time of the borrower's finance application.

Market maturity. What is the stage of maturity of the market (emerging, maturing or declining)? Typically, emerging or declining markets have the highest risk. Focus on the future and consider the likely market maturity when your development is scheduled to reach practical completion.

Market cyclicality. What is the impact of economic business cycles on the market? Generally, markets that are highly cyclical (or counter-cyclical) have higher risk. Consider the likely property market cycle when your development is due to reach practical completion.

Demand and supply analysis. Where a high degree of market risk exists in the property/development (i.e. there is a lower level of pre-commitments), provide evidence of the level of demand for the type of property in the relevant location and the level of competing supply.

Property market outlook. The assessor will comment on the outlook for the commercial property market. Focus on the same type and location as your subject property. Where possible, refer to independent market analysis/research.

Quality of securities

The following are some of the general issues that the assessor will consider:

- Is a Registered Mortgage Debenture/Floating Charge/Mortgage Debenture/Lien over the assets of the business borrower held or required? If so, is the value of these pledged assets quoted in the financial statements realistic and are they saleable?

▪ Are directors' guarantees held/appropriate? (Is there a statement of position of guarantors and their worth as guarantors? What is the realisable value of securities if sold?)

▪ Does the bank have effective control of the securities and are they readily saleable?

▪ Do the securities require monitoring (for obsolescence, market variations, nearby detrimental activities, environmental concerns, etc.), and if so, are appropriate covenants or conditions in place and known to you?

▪ Are there any preferential claims, subordination, retention of title or other conditions attached to any security (e.g. voting rights of other lenders/creditors, structural subordination)?

Securities for commercial property development lending – specific guidelines

The assessor will:

▪ Explain any proposed deviation from policy

▪ Comment on loan to cost ratio and explain any deviations from policy

- Ask whether the property is freehold or leasehold. If leasehold, terms of head lease/sublease(s) (e.g. start/end dates), current passing rent and rent review provisions (rent review dates and basis of reviews) should be detailed

- Advise as to whether a professional valuation has been obtained in accordance with Global Credit Policy, detailing:

  - Date of valuation

  - Whether valuation is from an approved valuer

  - Who instructed the valuer

  - Whether the valuation methodology is acceptable

- Confirm that the Relationship Manager has inspected the property securities (mandatory)

- Comment on ease of realisation, considering property location, alternative uses (if specialised property) and development status

- Comment on whether any planning issues or conditions, environmental issues or orders or other matters need to be addressed

- Detail insurance cover for the property

- Detail the contractor's all-risk insurance policy, including the limit of indemnity and expiry dates. Also detail claims history and current outstanding claims

- Comment on the borrower's capacity to fund cost overruns as and when they occur. If you do not have adequate capacity, guarantees/undertakings from the project sponsors or some other party of substance should be taken

- Confirm that the building contract is of a fixed time/fixed price nature

- Assess whether a tripartite (step-in) deed between the bank, the builder and the borrower (in respect of the building contract) is necessary.

Minimum security requirements

These include:

- Registered first-ranking charge over freehold/leasehold interest in the property

- Floating or registered mortgage debenture over the assets and undertakings of the borrower

- Personal guarantees of directors

- Appropriate cross-guarantees of associated entities

- Tripartite deeds relating to building contracts, sales contracts, agreements to lease (as appropriate)

- Charge over pre-sale contracts (including deposits) where appropriate.

The assessor is likely to make comments where these minimum requirements are not met.

Conditions precedent

Standard conditions precedent for property development lending are applied irrespective of loan details. The bank's managers are expected to incorporate all standard conditions into each new loan. Where individual conditions are not included, explanations are required.

Standard conditions precedent for commercial property development loans include:

- Builder and building contract must be acceptable to the bank – building contract to be executed

- Appropriate levels of pre-sales (normally between 80% and 120% of proposed debt) or pre-committed leases, depending on local conditions and project and market risk assessment

- The site is to be clear of contamination or other environmental problems. You will be expected to complete a satisfactory environmental questionnaire, with site investigation reports if deemed necessary

- The construction period should not exceed eighteen months

- An independent QS is to be retained for all building projects where construction costs exceed $1 million. A consulting engineer is required for all land subdivision projects where cost exceeds $1 million

- All progress payments/drawdowns under the facility should be made on a cost to complete basis

- Pre-commitment documentation (agreement for lease/lease or pre-sales contracts) is to be reviewed and be acceptable to the bank and its advisers

- Where pre-commitments feature, certification requires that the plans and specifications of the building contract accord with the plans and specifications of the pre-commitment documentation

- Professional valuation is to advise the value of the property 'as is', the value upon completion, feasibility of the project and demand/supply analysis. Minimum valuation amounts should be loan conditions

- A tripartite deed is required for larger or more complex projects

- Capitalisation of interest is permitted, but not after practical completion

- The borrower must demonstrate a capacity to fund cost overruns

- All acceptable insurances must be in place in relation to the development

- Confirmation that the contractor has sufficient levels of insurance in place (including public liability) is required

- One hundred per cent of net sales proceeds must be applied to the repayment of bank debt and reduction of limit

- Adverse material event covenants are to apply

- Construction is to commence within ninety days of issuance of letter of offer

- Shareholder or director contributions, where required, are to be made by way of share capital and/ or shareholder's/director's loans, repayment of which is to be formally postponed or subordinated to repayment of bank facilities

- A satisfactory search of relevant corporate registry records, in particular jurisdiction, is required.

Standard conditions precedent to the initial and each subsequent drawdown include:

- Certification from the independent quantity surveyor of:

  - Total expenditure to date on the project

  - Expenditure on the project since the date of the most recent drawdown

  - The cost to complete the project

  - The anticipated date of practical completion for the project

- Funds requested for drawdown shall not exceed expenditure on the scheme since the date of the most recent drawdown

- Cost to complete to be less than or equal to the funds available within the facility less the amount of the drawdown request before the bank. In the event that the cost to complete exceeds funds available within the facility, a cost overrun will be deemed to have occurred and no further debt funding will be permitted until the full amount of the cost overrun has been funded by additional equity

- Anticipated date of practical completion to be no later than the expiry date of the facility.

- Certification to be provided by the architect and relevant project consultants that actual construction is proceeding in accordance with the plans and specifications of the building contract

- Certification from the builder to be obtained confirming that all amounts due and payable to subcontractors, consultants, supplier and employees have been paid.

Covenants/ratios disciplines/conditions

A loan agreement is a contract between the bank and a customer that specifies the rights and obligations of each with regard to a certain loan or credit arrangement. It sets forth the conditions under which the loan is granted and establishes the parameters within which the borrower must operate.

A covenant is a clause in an agreement that specifies actions required (affirmative covenants) or prohibited (negative covenants). Covenants should be clearly defined and reasonable.

Covenants can do several things, including:

- Establishing a maximum ('...shall not exceed...')
- Forcing a minimum ('...shall not be less than...')
- Maintaining ('...shall not change...').

The overall purpose of establishing covenants, default provisions and remedy provisions is to give the bank the opportunity to act if the risk in a loan changes. A good covenant will be tight but will not interfere with a borrower's operations. Ratios should be sufficiently close to the actual or forecast position to ensure the covenant is breached in the event of a material deterioration in the financial position the covenant is designed to measure.

Covenants can be financial or non-financial in nature. Financial covenants usually address issues such as cash flow, profitability, efficiency, liquidity, solvency, capital structure and asset quality. Non-financial covenants will often assure full disclosure, management continuity and quality and the borrower's continued existence, and establish reporting requirements.

The credit assessor provides comment on the following, as applicable:

- The major covenants and ratio disciplines that will be relied upon and their adequacy or otherwise to mitigate key risks
- The historic performance of the borrower with regard to previously existing covenants, including

comments on any non-compliance and corrective actions taken during the period.

Non-financial covenants include:

■ Details of existing covenants with comments if the usual financial reporting covenants are not in place/proposed

■ An outline of the major covenants and ratio disciplines that will be relied upon and their adequacy or otherwise.

If a new covenant is added, the assessor will make comments as to what risk is to be negated by this covenant.

Covenants for commercial property development lending – specific guidelines

Conditions/covenants that should apply in all commercial property development loans include:

■ Minimum level and type of enforceable pre-commitments (pre-sales or pre-leases) required

■ Basis for equity contribution and payment of progress claims, specifying the required equity contributions and the timing of them (must be contributed in full prior to any bank funding being provided). All progress claims are to be paid on a cost to complete basis. Responsibility for cost overruns should be clearly stated. Funding will be permitted only where the cost to complete the development is less than or equal to the funds undrawn/available under the facility (less the amount of the progress payment/ drawdown request before the bank)

▪ Requirement for quantity surveyor/consulting engineer certification of progress claims. Appropriate certification from independent advisers must be received and be acceptable to the bank prior to payment of each progress claim

▪ The anticipated date of practical completion *must* be before the maturity date of the development loan facility.

Exit analysis

Comments will include a meaningful and realistic assessment of the sources of repayment or 'exits' available to the bank. The assessor will define such exit(s) showing how the bank can be repaid without loss under normal circumstances.

Primary exit. The primary source of repayment of a commercial property development loan will be the sale of the property/project at practical completion.

Sale of the property:

▪ The assessor will comment on the capacity to sell the property at completion

▪ In the normal course, the sale of the property should be pre-committed by a pre-sale agreement/contract (or a series of them for residential development) entered into before the development commences. This would be a condition precedent to funding

- For commercial property (office, retail and industrial), if a pre-sale does not exist, the likelihood of a sale occurring before or at completion should be assessed as a function of the level of lease pre-commitments in place and the investment market for the type of property being developed

- Where an element of market risk is involved (that is, where the level of pre-sales is less than the loan amount), assessors will comment in detail on the risk involved in securing additional sales during the development phase to enable repayment at loan maturity

- A break-even analysis should be conducted for the property/project

- The assessor will ask what percentage of the proposed debt facility is covered by pre-committed sales. What percentage of the unsold/uncommitted portion of the development needs to be sold (and at what price) to ensure repayment of bank debt?

The assessor will sensitise this analysis, considering the impact of less than 100% of pre-sales being settled. The completion percentage used for this sensitivity analysis will depend on an assessment of the settlement risk inherent in the project.

Secondary exit. A secondary exit is one that is not related to cash generated by the customer in the normal course of business.

The assessor will assess secondary exits provided by:

- Rental income, commenting on the ability to let the property and service/amortise the debt if the anticipated sales are not achieved
- Other assets/income of the borrower
- Other assets/income of guarantors or sponsors.

Property development finance can be challenging for the novice. I would recommend using a broker who has had the relevant experience in procuring property development funding for the type of development you're contemplating. Nevertheless, as a property developer you need to understand the fundamentals of property funding as this will determine the establishment of your project, including project structure, in the first instance.

Chapter 15

IT HAS TO SELL ITSELF

Marketing your project

When does the marketing for a project start? Is it when you have obtained the DA and are beginning your pre-sales? Is it when you begin construction or when you have completed the building?

I suggest your marketing should start the minute you create the vision for your development. If you return to the Development Site Sourcing Funnel™ introduced in Chapter 3, when you take that first step of choosing your location, at the same time consider the marketing aspects of your development: the target market, demographics, access to public transport and so forth. Assembling this type of information will help you to design a product that suits the market: 'What type of products will I build? If apartments, what sort of mix? Studio, one bedroom, two bedrooms, three bedrooms? Is on-site car parking required? Must it conform to council regulations or can I choose how many spaces to include?' All this market information gathering is part of the due diligence and will feed into the project's feasibility analysis.

Remember, marketing does not start with approval of the DA, when you decide to have a real estate agent create some brochures and a website. *It starts on day one and it starts with you.*

The other critical factor that impacts on your marketing strategy is the bank's funding criteria as discussed in the previous chapter. These days the bank will typically require 100% pre-sales before it will allow you to draw down on the loan for construction costs. This does not mean you have to sell all of your apartments; it means you have to sell enough to cover 100% of your borrowings. You may, for example, cover 100% of your debt by selling 50% of your units. Sometimes, depending on your risk profile, the bank may require 110% pre-sales.

It is important to understand the effect that pre-sales will have on your sales revenue and therefore your profit –

and, more importantly, your risk margin. As we discussed in Chapter 14, pre-sales mean you have *fixed inflows* and *increasing outflows*. So you have locked in your sales revenue (inflow), or a large portion of it, before the start of construction, and of course the development costs (outflow) will continue to grow. This can be very risky, particularly if the market turns and you cannot recoup the discounts on your pre-sales from sales of your remaining units on completion.

Finally, you must select a competent project marketing agent who knows your target market and is experienced in delivering an effective marketing plan.

Provided you have done your due diligence as developer and meet the market with the right type and quality of product, and provided the marketing plan is executed professionally and efficiently, the sales campaign will be successful. The goal is to build up a sufficient number of qualified prospects so that, come Launch Day, you are oversubscribed and sell out within a weekend.

Fundamentals of a marketing plan
for residential apartments

What	When
Website, computer renditions, virtual tours (create and build expectations)	Post-design development phase
Expressions of interest (often including refundable fee) and lead capture	Once DA has been lodged
Social media activities	Once DA has been lodged
Magazines and other real estate media	Once DA has been lodged
Sales collateral, pricing strategy and lists, brochures, finishes boards, specifications	Prior to launch
Sales office	Prior to launch
Launch Day	For qualified prospects

Chapter 16

HOW AND WHEN DO I GET OUT?

Exit strategies

Your exit strategies will vary depending on your personal situation and on market conditions. Other decisive factors will be your level of experience, financial circumstances and risk profile, and whether or not you have managed your project well.

It is extremely important that exit strategies are planned comprehensively and well before any money is committed. Once you have completed your preliminary financial feasibility analysis, identify your exit points. You might base these on an 'early harvest', where you on-sell the development after having added some value and taken a profit while leaving enough in the deal for it still to be attractive to an incoming developer. Typically these exit points will be after an option agreement has been signed and a buyer has been lined up to buy the option, or after the DA has been approved and the value of the land has increased significantly. Securing sites, adding value and on-selling in this way is a business in its own right, and there are a number of small site acquisition businesses that operate very successfully under this model. You could undertake this activity on an ongoing basis as a cash flow strategy.

Alternatively you may have predetermined exit strategies as contingency, for example:

- If some of your finished apartments are not selling at the right price, you may wish to refinance and rent them

- If you are unable to obtain pre-sales within a reasonable period of time, as dictated by your Feasibility, you may wish to sell the project

- If the approved DA is less than expected and falls below your hurdle rate, you may wish to sell at that point.

Other considerations when planning your exit strategies will be your investors, joint venture partners and funders. These stakeholders will be impacted positively or otherwise whichever strategy you employ. It is prudent therefore to ensure that your legal documentation provides you with the flexibility to exit at will and not be constrained to the detrement of your project's financial outcome. Indeed, it is difficult if not impossible to gain agreement for joint ventures and secure funds from investors, if clear exit strategies are not outlined at the very beginning of negotiations.

The essential point about exit strategies is to ensure you have a *planned* exit rather than resorting to a *forced* exit, which will always make it more difficult to realise a profit.

Chapter 17

THE PROOF OF THE PUDDING IS IN THE EATING

The Apprentice Property Developer Masterclass

As I mentioned early in the book, I have taught property development to many thousands of budding entrepreneurs through my Property Development Workshops, which I founded in 2004. Over many years I have received one common and persistent request from the graduates: they wanted me to hold their hand, so to speak, and mentor them through a property development project from start to finish. Depending on the project and the exit strategy, this could take anything from twelve months to a number of years.

Two years ago I decided to accept the challenge. I would ask for expressions of interest from all graduates of the three-day workshop and select a team of between five and seven individuals to complete a project in Sydney. This would put into practice the theory already learned at the workshop and enable participants to experience a guided property development project as part of a team and as a director in their own property development company. The goal would be to transform each participant into a successful property development entrepreneur.

The project objectives are as follows:

- Complete one project from start to finish
- Achieve a minimum development profit margin of 30% on completion
- Achieve a minimum ROI for each participant of 50–150%
- Capture learnings through each phase of the development process
- Operate a successful property development business
- Document the project along the way to facilitate future learnings and projects.

The project is undertaken using the 7-Phase Property Development Process methodology taught in my three-day Property Development Workshop, as follows:

Phase 1: source development site and establish project viability:

- Source a development site
- Technical analysis
- Financial feasibility analysis
- Financial modelling and project funding
- Project legal structure
- Sales and marketing strategies
- Exit strategy
- Establishing a business plan.

Phase 2: site negotiations and acquisition:

- Options
- JVs.

Phase 3: approval process:

- DA process
- CC (construction certificate).

Phase 4: construction process:

- Tender documentation
- Tender for builder

- ▪ Manage construction
- ▪ Cost management
- ▪ Project management/contract administration.

Phase 5: sales and marketing:

- ▪ Execute predetermined strategies.

Phase 6: exit strategies:

- ▪ Execute predetermined strategies.

Phase 7: project evaluation:

- ▪ Group performance analysis.

The first Apprentice Property Developer Masterclass (APDM) was completed in 2015 and was a resounding success. The team achieved the following results:

- ▪ Profit for each of the seven participants ranged from $1.1 million to $1.4 million (on top of their original investment)
- ▪ ROI averaged well over 400%.

The Property Development Workshop methodology worked perfectly and the participants have now gone on to undertake their own projects. Some have since quit their jobs to do property development full time.

APDM 2 and 3 are currently underway.

A large part of the success of the APDM Team 1 can be attributed to "My ten principles for developing property successfully" which I would like to share with you:

1. As an aspiring developer, educate yourself *before* attempting a property development project

2. Find the right site by applying a predetermined list of criteria. Do not compromise on the quality or price of the site

3. Establish your minimum hurdle rate (risk margin) and stick to it no matter what. Avoid the temptation to massage the financial feasibility to 'make it work'

4. Establish an appropriate legal structure to minimise liabilities and maximise profit

5. Use as little of your own money as possible. Always be investor-ready and fundable

6. Assemble a star team and not a team of stars. Know how to choose your consultants. Professional support for the duration is critical

7. Choose your builder carefully and help them to help you

8. Know who *all* your stakeholders are and take their interests into consideration when planning your development. Don't underestimate the power of the neighbours

9. Always have the right intent when deciding to do a development. It's not just about making money. Have a bigger vision and make a real contribution to the community

10. Know your why. Your mindset is critical and will determine whether you fail or succeed. Property development is not just doing one project; it's a business. You have to become the CEO of a property development business, with all the responsibilities and accountabilities that entails.

SUMMARY

As developer, you are responsible and accountable for the success of your project. You are empowered to *make happen*. You are the difference between success and failure.

Your level of success is intrinsically linked and commensurate to your level of education in the field of property development. You can be the biggest risk in your project, unless you take the necessary steps to make yourself project-ready.

So what do you need to do?

Well, congratulations! You have completed the first step by reading this book. Education and your own personal development are the keys to your success.

One of the first things to do is take a skills inventory of yourself. Identify all the skills you have acquired working over the years and during your studies. Then do a SWOT analysis to identify your strengths, weaknesses, opportunities and threats. Remember, strengths and weaknesses are internal factors, and opportunities and threats are external factors over which you may have less control. This exercise will help you identify those areas where you will require support and is therefore critical when selecting consultants and advisers.

Getting Started

Your Property Development Business Plan

Now you have learned the 7-Phase Property Development Process and the risks associated with each phase, and those that you may pose as a developer, you are well armed to do your business plan. This will force you to think through all the issues carefully and address them accordingly. It will also help you identify your goals and your 'why'. It is important for you to identify your broader vision for doing property development (beyond just making money or creating wealth).

Typically, the table of contents for your business plan should include:

- Executive summary
- Description of your property development business
- Legal structure
- Your team
- SWOT analysis
- Goals and objectives
- Finance and budgets.

Appendices:

- Project plan no. 1
- Project description
- Time frames
- Site sourcing
- Site negotiations and acquisition
  - Options
  - JVs
- Legal structure
- Project team
- Development approval
- Builder selection
- Construction
- Marketing and sales
- Exit strategies.

Interview With Jim Castagnet, Author, MD And Founder, Property Development Workshops

▪ *Who is Jim Castagnet and what do you do?*

I am a property developer and have been developing high-end residential and mixed-use property since 1998, when I orchestrated my escape from the corporate world of telecommunications.

After a number of challenging years developing and guest speaking at the University of Western Sydney's (CALE) property course, I founded Property Development Workshops (PDW) in 2004.

▪ *What does Property Development Workshops provide?*

I teach aspiring entrepreneurs how to create private wealth through developing residential and mixed-use property safely and for maximum profit.

▪ *Who are your clients?*

I cater for individuals who generally have a deep passion for property and want to create wealth developing it. They understand that 75% of Australia's rich-listers, and the world's for that matter, have created and/or hold their wealth in property. At my half-day 'Introduction to Property Development' seminars, I typically find I have a roomful of some 100 or so budding entrepreneurs and professionals who are keen to learn about the development industry. My goal is to educate and transform them into successful property developers.

■ **What problems do you solve for them?**

Property development sits in the highest risk category of all industries, and has one of the highest failure rates. But most often the risk factor is not the project itself, but the developer. By that I mean the developer is ill-prepared because of a lack of knowledge and experience, and one reason for this is the difficulty in extracting information from what is a very 'closed' industry in which the secrets are well guarded. This problem is exacerbated by the fact that most of the property development deals that are done involve a confidentiality agreement that precludes developers and consultants from divulging any information.

At Property Development Workshops I pride myself on delivering all the necessary knowledge and insights the developer needs to be able to undertake a project that involves minimum risk, maximum profit and, not least, an enjoyable, enriching experience for the developer.

■ **How are you able to do this? What makes you different?**

Property Development Workshops is unique for a number of reasons. Firstly, I provide comprehensive property development education and not a get-rich-quick scheme.

Secondly, drawing on my eighteen years as a developer, I have established a consistently successful methodology, my 7-Phase Property Development Process, which I set out and dissect in the workshop. This process provides a framework that can be easily followed and implemented by the prospective developer.

Thirdly, as a practising developer, I use real-life case studies of my past projects, and significantly I also survey my current projects, as each one provides unique learning opportunities.

Finally, 'the proof of the pudding is in the eating'. My unique 'Apprentice Property Developer Masterclass' is by invitation only and entails a selection process. Each year I take on a group of five to seven graduates from the three-day Property Development Workshop program and mentor them through a real-life development project, from start to finish, to ensure they successfully complete the project and maximise their profit. It's the ultimate on the job training opportunity: learn and make a huge profit at the same time!

▪ *I'm thinking of attending the workshop. How can I be sure you will be able to provide me with the knowledge I need to start developing?*

I have been developing mid-level to high-end residential property in Sydney's Eastern Suburbs, arguably the riskiest market in Australia, since 1998. I have been running the educational Property Development Workshops since 2004, before which I presented at the University of Western Sydney for two years in their Business School property course as a newbie developer.

The workshop features seven other presenters in both Sydney and Melbourne, including a property lawyer, an architect, a property finance specialist, property accountant, a department of planning and council executive, a valuer and a quantity surveyor, along with other guests property developers, all of whom share their knowledge and expertise. The information you receive at this educational forum is unique in both quantity and quality.

In the early stages of my career I learned many of the inherent difficulties of building a property development business by trial and error, so I know well how it feels to lack the support and information that are essential for success, which is why I decided to create this workshop. By openly sharing my experiences (the good, the bad and the ugly) in the workshop, I can help other prospective developers build their own essential skill set.

■ *How do your graduates feel after they have completed the Property Development Workshop?*

I have been pleasantly surprised, not so much by the number of attendees I have helped since 2004, but rather by who has attended. They have included industry leaders, large corporate executives, government officials, university lecturers, all manner of consultants and professionals, small business owners and entrepreneurs, including a BRW rich-lister.

But more importantly the majority of my students are "ordinary" people who have no previous real estate experience but are keen to get into the industry and create private wealth for themselves and family.

I am humbled by the written testimonials from past participants, some of which I have posted on the website. I am currently helping one of the biggest international companies in Australia to maximise their property portfolio.

Numerous graduates have gone on to build their own successful careers. One who attended in 2004 recently presented his latest projects in Sydney's Northern Beaches at the workshop.

Graduates who complete the workshop consistently feel empowered, knowing that they hold their destiny in their own hands, that they can achieve success, gaining both wealth and independence through their property development business.

▪ *So what's your mission?*
I want to be recognised, both here and overseas, as one of Australia's most innovative and successful property developers who also happens to deliver the industry's number one 'must-do' educational property development workshop.

Acknowledgements

I would like to thank my team members and consultants who are very much part of the PDW family and without whom I would not have achieved so much.

Stephan Castagnet, General Manager, PDW, who carries the wisdom of an old man on such young shoulders. You are a godsend.

Gerard Gooden, Lawyer, your wisdom, guidance and dedication to 'the cause' of providing property development education have been invaluable over the 16 or so years we have been working together. You have been a tower of strength.

David Gurney, Accountant, you are the voice of reason in a world full of uncertainty. I can always count on you to provide clarity and make sense of any situation

Stan Fitzroy-Mendis, Town Planner, whose support has been invaluable at our property development workshops for countless number of years

The PDW team, you are the backbone of our organistaion and we could not do it without you

Patricia Castagnet, Office Manager

Lana Shelest, Sales & Marketing Manager

Alicia-Rose Castagnet, Executive Assistant

The Author

Jim has over 20 years' experience successfully developing residential and mixed-use residential property. After spending two years as a guest presenter at University of Western Sydney's Business School's property course, Jim founded Property Development Workshops, a property development education company, in 2004

Jim has a Post Graduate Diploma in Urban Estate Management (Property Economics) from University of Technology, Sydney. He is a well-respected industry leader and whilst always engaged in developing, he makes time to share his knowledge through his Workshops and Masterclasses, presents regularly at Business Functions and Study Groups, and has featured on Sky Business Real Estate News Programme.

Jim's passion for property development is such that he has made it his mission to help as many entrepreneurs as possible to succeed in this extremely challenging but equally rewarding industry.

For more information about Jim and
Property Development Workshops, visit:
www.propertydevelopmentworkshops.com.au

Made in the USA
Middletown, DE
13 December 2021